Solo Serenatas

RECENT RESEARCHES IN MUSIC

A-R Editions publishes seven series of critical editions, spanning the history of Western music, American music, and oral traditions.

RECENT RESEARCHES IN THE MUSIC OF THE MIDDLE AGES AND EARLY RENAISSANCE
   Charles M. Atkinson, general editor

RECENT RESEARCHES IN THE MUSIC OF THE RENAISSANCE
   James Haar, general editor

RECENT RESEARCHES IN THE MUSIC OF THE BAROQUE ERA
   Steven Saunders, general editor

RECENT RESEARCHES IN THE MUSIC OF THE CLASSICAL ERA
   Neal Zaslaw, general editor

RECENT RESEARCHES IN THE MUSIC OF THE NINETEENTH AND EARLY TWENTIETH CENTURIES
   Rufus Hallmark, general editor

RECENT RESEARCHES IN AMERICAN MUSIC
   John M. Graziano, general editor

RECENT RESEARCHES IN THE ORAL TRADITIONS OF MUSIC
   Philip V. Bohlman, general editor

Each edition in *Recent Researches* is devoted to works by a single composer or to a single genre. The content is chosen for its high quality and historical importance and is edited according to the scholarly standards that govern the making of all reliable editions.

For information on establishing a standing order to any of our series, or for editorial guidelines on submitting proposals, please contact:

A-R Editions, Inc.
Middleton, Wisconsin

800 736-0070 (North American book orders)
608 836-9000 (phone)
608 831-8200 (fax)
http://www.areditions.com

RECENT RESEARCHES IN THE MUSIC OF THE BAROQUE ERA, 175

Alessandro Scarlatti

Solo Serenatas

Edited by Marie-Louise Catsalis
and Rosalind Halton

A-R Editions, Inc.
Middleton, Wisconsin

Performance parts are available from the publisher.

A-R Editions, Inc., Middleton, Wisconsin
© 2011 by A-R Editions, Inc.

All rights reserved. No part of this book may be reproduced or transmitted in any form by any electronic or mechanical means (including photocopying, recording, or information storage and retrieval) without permission in writing from the publisher.

The purchase of this edition does not convey the right to perform it in public, nor to make a recording of it for any purpose. Such permission must be obtained in advance from the publisher.

A-R Editions is pleased to support scholars and performers in their use of *Recent Researches* material for study or performance. Subscribers to any of the *Recent Researches* series, as well as patrons of subscribing institutions, are invited to apply for information about our "Copyright Sharing Policy."

Printed in the United States of America

ISBN 978-0-89579-712-4
ISSN 0484-0828

♾ The paper used in this publication meets the minimum requirements of the American National Standard for Information Sciences—Permanence of Paper for Printed Library Materials, ANSI Z39.48-1992.

Contents

Abbreviations   viii

Acknowledgments   ix

Historical Introduction, *Marie-Louise Catsalis*   xi

    Defining the Solo Serenata   xii
    Common Features of Solo Serenatas   xv
    Notes   xviii

Musical Style and Performance, *Rosalind Halton*   xxiii

    Tonal Structure   xxiii
    Aria Types   xxv
    Recurrent Elements in Scarlatti's Solo Serenatas   xxvi
    Aspects of Performance   xxvi
    Notes   xxix

Texts and Translations   xxxi

Plates   xliii

Serenate a voce sola

Sventurati miei penzieri: Serenata a voce sola di canto

    [Arioso e Recitativo]—[Aria]: "Sventurati miei penzieri"—"Se taccio, se parlo"   2

Eurilla, amata Eurilla: Serenata a voce sola

    1. [Recitativo]: "Eurilla, amata Eurilla"   9
    2. [Aria]: "Come mai partir potrò"   10
    3. Recitativo: "Ma barbaro spietato"   11
    4. [Aria]: "Lungi ancor dal petto amante"   12
    5. [Recitativo]: "Eurilla, anima mia"   14

All'hor che stanco il sole: Serenata a voce sola [con violini]

    1. [Sinfonia]   15
    2. [Recitativo]: "All'hor che stanco il sole"   16
    3. [Aria]: " 'Clori bella, e dove sei?' "   18
    4. [Aria]: "Se del Tebro in su le sponde"   21
    5. [Recitativo]: "Misero, a che son giunto?"   23
    6. [Aria]: "Deh, torna mia vita"   24
    7. [Recitativo]: "Ma con chi parlo?"   26
    8. [Aria]: "Aure placide e serene"   26
    9. [Recitativo]: "E dite alla crudel"   28
    10. [Aria]: " 'Già che more un disperato' "   29
    11. [Aria]: "Ma se mosse a pietà"   31
    12. [Recitativo]—[Aria]: "Bastan l'amante luci"—"S'alla bocca del caro mio bene"   33
    13. [Recitativo]: "O fallaci speranze"   35

Hor che l'aurato nume: Serenata a voce sola con violini

1. Sonata   37
2. [Recitativo]: "Hor che l'aurato nume"   39
3. Aria: "Se in amor col dolce incanto"   40
4. Aria: "Fu il tuo bel un tuono"   42
5. Aria: "Ah! nascondi il tuo rigore"   44
6. [Aria]: "Se non vuoi ch'io t'ami"   46
7. [Aria]: "Alle sponde dell'onde di Lethe"   49
8. Recitativo: "Sì, sì, fuggi cor mio"   51
9. [Aria]: "Ah! fiera sorte"   53

Prima d'esservi infedele: Serenata a voce sola con violini

1. [Introdutione]: "Prima d'esservi infedele"   55
2. Recitativo: "Ma se con bella fede"   59
3. Aria: "Quando sorge l'aurora"   60
4. [Recitativo]: "Lieta, lieta così"   63
5. Aria: "Se la sorte avesse in seno"   64
6. Recitativo: "Esempio di costanza"   71

Perché tacete, regolati concenti?: Cantata, alto solo con violini

1. Sinfonia   73
2. [Recitativo]: "Perché tacete, regolati concenti?"   78
3. Aria: "Alla mano che dotta in voi scherza"   79
4. [Recitativo]: "Ma che dissi? Tacete!"   82
5. [Aria]: "Tra le fiamme del mio duolo"   82
6. [Recitativo]: "Nè m'ascolti, crudele"   87
7. [Aria]: "Dormi, ma sappi almen"   88
8. [Recitativo]: "Ma tiranna, tu dormi"   90
9. [Aria]: "Deh pensieri"   91

Sotto l'ombra d'un faggio: Serenata a voce sola con violini

1. [Introdutione]: "Sotto l'ombra d'un faggio"   95
2. Aria: "Scioglietemi, lasciatemi"   98
3. Recitativo: "Pietà, pietà lasciate!"   100
4. Aria: "Io dormivo presso al rivo"   101
5. Recitativo: "Ragione ha il cor"   105
6. Aria: "Talvolta il dolore"   106

Notte, ch'in carro d'ombre: Serenata, soprano solo con violini

1. [Introdutione]   109
2. [Recitativo]: "Notte, ch'in carro d'ombre"   111
3. [Aria]: "Vieni, o Notte"   112
4. [Recitativo]: "E tu, ch'ognor ti vanti"   116
5. [Aria]: "Veloce e labile"   117
6. Recitativo: "Ma parmi ch'esaudite"   121
7. [Aria]: "Con l'idea d'un bel gioire"   122
8. [Recitativo]: "Ma voi non vi chiudete"   126
9. [Aria]: "Sì che priva di contento"   127

Hor che di Febo ascosi: Serenata, soprano solo con violini

    1. Introdutione   132
    2. Recitativo: "Hor che di Febo ascosi"   133
    3. Aria: "Cara notte"   134
    4. Recitativo: "Ma chi m'addita"   139
    5. Aria: "Sì, sì, non dormite"   140
    6. Recitativo: "Quindi dai vostri sguardi"   143
    7. Aria: "Vago fior, ch'in notte algente"   144
    8. Recitativo: "Ma no, riposa o bella"   150
    9. Aria: "Dormite, posate"   151

Critical Report   155

    Sources   155
    Editorial Methods   159
    Critical Notes   160
    Notes   164

Appendix: *Era l'oscura notte*   167

The Authorship of *Era l'oscura notte*   168

    Notes   168

Text and Translation   169

Era l'oscura notte: Serenata a voce sola con strumenti

    1. [Recitativo]: "Era l'oscura notte"   171
    2. Aria: " 'Lo vedrai s'io son fedele o crudele' "   173
    3. Recitativo: " 'E dove, amato bene' "   178
    4. Aria: " 'Se penso al caro ben' "   178
    5. Recitativo: " 'E mai lungi da te' "   183
    6. Aria: " 'Fu costante di Tirsi la fede' "   183
    7. Recitativo: " 'Così è pentita allora' "   186
    8. Aria: " 'Amerai ma sol quell'ombra' "   186

Source and Critical Notes   191

Abbreviations

B-Bc	Conservatoire royal de Bruxelles, Bibliothèque, Belgium
D-Dl	Dresden, Sächsische Landesbibliothek – Staats- und Universitätsbibliothek, Germany
D-MÜs	Münster, Santini-Bibliothek, Germany
F-Pc	Conservatoire de Paris, Bibliothèque, France
F-Pn	Paris, Bibliothèque nationale de France, Département de la Musique, France
GB-CDp	Cardiff Public Libraries, Central Library, U.K.
GB-Lam	London, Royal Academy of Music, U.K.
GB-Lbl	London, British Library, U.K.
GB-Lcm	London, Royal College of Music, U.K.
GB-Och	Oxford, Christ Church College Library, U.K.
I-Bc	Museo internazionale e biblioteca della musica di Bologna, Italy
I-MC	Archivio dell'Abbazia di Montecassino, Italy
I-PAc	Parma, Conservatorio di Musica A. Boito, Biblioteca, Italy
I-Fas	Archivio di Stato di Firenze, Biblioteca, Italy
I-Fc	Florence, Conservatorio Statale di Musica Luigi Cherubini, Biblioteca, Italy
I-Nc	Naples, Conservatorio di Musica San Pietro a Majella, Biblioteca, Italy
I-Rvat	Rome, Biblioteca Apostolica Vaticana, Italy
US-BEm	Jean Gray Hargrove Music Library, University of California, Berkeley, U.S.A.
US-NH, Osb.	New Haven, Connecticut, Irving S. Gilmore Music Library, Yale University, James M. Osborn Collection, U.S.A.

Acknowledgments

We acknowledge with deep gratitude the generous assistance of the following librarians in supplying copies and giving permission to use the manuscript sources of the serenatas: Dr. Mauro Amato, Biblioteca del Conservatorio di Musica San Pietro a Majella, Naples; Don Faustino Avagliano, Archivio dell'Abbazia di Montecassino; Dr. Gianni Ciabbatini, Biblioteca del Conservatorio Statale di Musica Luigi Cherubini, Florence; Barbara Glowka, Librarian of the Diözesanbibliothek, Münster; Federica Riva, Biblioteca del Conservatorio di Musica, Parma; Catherine Massip, Bibliothèque nationale, Paris; staff of the British Library, London; staff of the Royal College of Music, London; staff of the Conservatoire royal de Bruxelles; staff of the Museo internazionale e biblioteca della musica di Bologna; staff of the Sächsische Landesbibliothek, Dresden; and the staff of Biblioteca Apostolica Vaticana, Rome.

Friends and colleagues who have generously answered questions, solved editorial problems, and enriched our research in the field of Scarlatti's solo serenatas include: Dr. Kathryn Bosi, Morrill Music Librarian, Biblioteca Berenson, I Tatti, Florence; Professor Biancamaria Brumana, Università degli Studi di Perugia; Professor Lowell Lindgren, MIT; Dr. Guido Olivieri, University of Texas at Austin; and Professor Alexander Silbiger, Duke University and editor of the Web Library of Seventeenth-Century Music.

This edition owes a great deal to the tireless energy of our text editors and translators: Nerida Newbigin, Emeritus Professor of Italian Studies, University of Sydney; Barbara Sachs, Loro Ciuffenna; and Marie Bertola, Santa Clara University. Many thanks also to Professor Peter Burian for his contributions to the initial translation process, and to Professor Danilo Romei, Università di Firenze, and Roberto Pagano, Palermo, for most helpful advice in clarifying detailed points of the texts and translations.

Many performers in Australia and the U.S., both student and professional, have played an essential part in this edition, by discovering with us these beautiful and in most cases unknown works. These include singers Tamsin Simmill (*Sventurati miei penzieri* and *Eurilla, amata Eurilla*), Jennifer Kaye (*Eurilla, amata Eurilla*), Anna Sandstrom (*Hor che l'aurato nume*), Dan Cromeenes (*Perché tacete, regolati concenti?*), Nancy Wait-Kromm (*Sotto l'ombra d'un faggio*), and Joelene Griffith (*Notte, ch'in carro d'ombre*); and instrumentalists Matthew Bruce, Elizabeth Pogson, Kate Morgan, Tommie Andersson, Claudia Bloom, Ryo Fukuda, Peter Gelfand, and Bruce Moyer.

We acknowledge with thanks funding from the Faculty-Student Research Assistant Research Program at Santa Clara University, which made possible the participation of research students Katie Brennan and Kelly O'Donnell; also the administrative assistance of Rob Kathner at Santa Clara University Music Department. Thank you also to Vivienne Boon and the music library staff of the University of Newcastle, Australia, for their support, and to Tomoyo Ueda, Bremerhaven, for valued research assistance.

We acknowledge with thanks the Research Management Committee of the University of Newcastle, 1999–2005, which supported the recording *Venere, Adone e Amore: Serenatas and Cantatas by Alessandro Scarlatti* (ABC Classics 476 6170, 2007), including the performance of *Hor che di Febo ascosi* by Jane Edwards (soprano) and *chacona* (Lucinda Moon and Stephen Freeman, violins; Jamie Hey, Rosemary Webber, and Tommie Anderson, basso continuo; director and harpsichord, Rosalind Halton).

Lastly, an enormous debt of gratitude is owed to our husbands, Grant Parker and David Halton, respectively, for their tireless love and support, and especially for all the driving!

Historical Introduction

Marie-Louise Catsalis

Alessandro Scarlatti was the most prolific and arguably the greatest composer of solo cantatas in his day. According to Edwin Hanley's 1963 thematic catalogue of his solo cantatas, 783 are extant.[1] Thomas E. Griffin identifies eight of these works as having the additional (or sole) designation "serenata."[2] To these I have added two, based on their title pages, and these ten works are presented in this edition. It is likely that of Scarlatti's impressive oeuvre of cantatas, several others may also have functioned as solo serenatas. However, until further evidence from the period comes to light, these are the only ones we can be sure were considered to be serenatas by at least the poet, composer, copyist, or patron, or a combination of all four.

The term "serenata" has been linked to such a wide variety of works that it is not easy to gain clarity concerning the genre. It is necessary to view it in relation to the major vocal genres of the period, namely the oratorio, opera, and cantata. If we use these other genres to form subcategories, we arrive at a division between the oratorical, dramatic, and solo serenata.[3] Whereas the oratorical serenata was an ostentatious display of power in the form of a secular oratorio, and the dramatic serenata was a miniature opera probably intended for bourgeois consumption, the solo serenata was performed for smaller, more intimate gatherings, such as the *conversazioni* held at various learned academies—including the Roman Accademia dell'Arcadia, to which Alessandro Scarlatti was admitted in 1706.[4] These were occasions at which the *litterati* gathered: poets, musicians, artists, and orators, in order to discuss matters of artistic importance. One reason that references to the solo serenata are rare is that, like the solo cantata, its audience was limited in number and essentially private: this chamber genre is a sophisticated one, aimed at the cognoscenti.[5]

With new editions of serenatas appearing, it is the large-scale serenatas that have been given attention,[6] whereas the existence of the solo serenata has tended to be subsumed within the larger genre of solo cantata. Roger Freitas investigates the solo cantata from the point of view of its reception within this circle of extremely well-educated listeners, who often doubled as composer or poet or singer.[7] He states that during the seventeenth century, "as the European nobility gradually abandoned its traditional warrior function during the Renaissance . . . it relied increasingly on behaviour and style as markers of superiority. . . . [S]ocial interaction could take on the character of a fiercely competitive struggle, now not of arms but of fashion and manners."[8] Keeping this in mind, the text and the music was often seen as a clever exchange, highly mannered, and always presenting a challenge to the next pretender. Under these circumstances, allusions to specific occasions or dedications to honored members were not likely to be blatantly obvious. With such subtlety a given part of the art, and in an almost secret gathering of elite members, it is not surprising that three centuries later, allusions to celebrated events escape the modern scholar. It has also been documented that the texts of cantatas given in the academies were synopses of academic debates.[9] Certainly here the link to the oratorical serenata is evident, in which the debate element of the text is a vital ingredient of the text, in place of a dramatic narrative.

There still remains, however, considerable confusion and overlap between the solo serenata and the solo cantata during the seventeenth and early eighteenth centuries, and it is likely that "cantata" and "serenata" were somewhat interchangeable terms. Alessandro Scarlatti's solo serenatas, identified as such on their title pages, are as follows (H indicates the number given by Hanley in his 1963 thematic catalogue of cantatas): H. 33, *All'hor che stanco il sole*; H. 249, *Era l'oscura notte*; H. 252, *Eurilla, amata Eurilla*; H. 480, *Notte, ch'in carro d'ombre*; H. 511, *Hor che di Febo ascosi*; H. 516, *Hor che l'aurato nume*; H. 551, *Perchè tacete, regolati concenti?*; H. 578, *Prima d'esservi infedele*; H. 678, *Sotto l'ombra d'un faggio*; and H. 710, *Sventurati miei penzieri*. It is likely that many more of the cantatas were used for serenata occasions but cannot be identified as such. For example, a work for soprano solo and two violins by Antonio Farina, on a text beginning "Sovra carro stellato," is entitled "Serenata" in Ms. I-Nc 33.4.4. A work with the same incipit attributed to Alessandro Scarlatti is termed "Cantata" in the source I-Nc 34.5.10 and 11. Further investigation is warranted as to whether the solo serenata can be differentiated to a greater degree, either by textual or musical elements, from the solo cantata. It is hoped that the presentation of these works in a single volume will begin to define the solo serenata as a recognized performance genre of the period.

Defining the Solo Serenata

The solo serenata has the strongest links back to the Renaissance serenata, from which the whole genre adopts its name. Griffin says:

> At the same time that the large occasional cantata or serenata of explicit political import enjoyed a vogue in Italy, the older custom of the amorous, intimate serenade in a lady's honor continued to be observed.[10]

Michael Talbot reviews the many and varied uses of the word serenata over nearly four centuries and comes up with three broad definitions, of which the following is the first:

> The Song by a lover to his beloved. This genre straddles the boundary between art and folk music and is not specific to any period. Nor can it be defined, in art music at least, by the use of particular performing forces or musical structures. Its identity is established rather by context and purpose.[11]

Dinko Fabris examines the term serenata as defined in lexicons of the period and attributes the prevalence of the form in Naples to the fact that it can be poetically linked with that city's symbol "la Sirena."[12] He cites several manuscripts of works with the designation "serenata," and the genre is particularly well represented in the mid- to late-seventeenth century. All of the works have in common the presence of obbligato violins, and above all, the text creates a soothing nocturnal atmosphere to calm the sorrows of love.

One contemporary German writer,[13] Johann Mattheson, also speaks of serenatas as intimate nighttime pieces. He objects to the use of the term to denote large ensemble pieces for political occasions, emphasizing instead the smaller-scale chamber setting, with one to two voices:

> Of secular vocal pieces outside the theater, the serenata or night music (for one or more voices, always with instruments) has deserved superiority....
>
> The chief characteristic of the serenata must always be tenderness, *la tendresse*. I say the chief characteristic, for in this genre there are also very many marginal circumstances. Cantatas, each in its own way, employ various emotions and passions, only one however at a time, and present them in a narrative, story-telling fashion. Serenatas as a whole, however, require primarily nothing but tender, strong love, by which the poet must be guided if he desires to apprehend their correct nature. There must be no melody so small nor piece so large that a chief mark of distinction does not assuredly prevail before and above others in it, clearly distinguishing it from the others. Otherwise it means little or nothing.
>
> Accordingly, it runs counter to the very nature of the serenata if one makes use of it, so to speak, outside its own element (I refer to the affection) at congratulatory celebrations, official pageantry, graduation ceremonies etc. Political and military occasions are alien to its nature, for the night is not connected with anything else in such tender intimacy as with love and sleep. The other occasions are served by oratorios and aubades and all kinds of morning music, and have as characteristics some splendid, bombastic and rousing traits which would hardly be appropriate for tenderness and secret stirrings of the heart. Thus an oratorio needs more voices, while a solo singer or a pair of voices suffices for a serenata, which is again a good feature.[14]

Griffin makes the following observations on this definition:

> Mattheson's discussion of the serenata is the most detailed written by any seventeenth- or eighteenth-century theorist, yet it is not without its faults. Love and tenderness may well have been the chief characteristics of the amorous serenata below a lady's balcony, and in fact they are prominent in the two-voice serenatas of Alessandro Scarlatti, but Mattheson's observation that these qualities were the hallmark of all such works is not confirmed by historical evidence. Mattheson himself is known to have composed a number of serenatas, and at least one of them, *Die Frohlockende Themse*, appears to contradict his own assertion as to the nature of this genre.[15]

To present a contrary view, Mattheson acknowledges the existence of the large political serenata, and interestingly refers to it as an oratorio. However, he has a preference for the small, intimate "serenata" for one or two voices, as it is more appropriate to the night setting and the original intention of the genre. According to the work-list in *New Grove*, Mattheson wrote eighteen Italian secular cantatas, various secular wedding cantatas, and serenades.[16] So, as Griffin says, it is true that Mattheson composed large ceremonial serenatas, but the smaller, more intimate variety commissioned by members of the bourgeoisie also appear in his output. We must remember that the musician in this period was the servant of the patron, and it was the employer whose wishes were paramount. The impact of the patron regarding serenata forms must be kept in mind constantly by serenata scholars.

The question remains: what could the title "serenata" mean in the context of the solo cantata? It is relevant at this point to heed the advice of Carolyn Gianturco when she writes the following regarding genre division:

> To the unproblematic state of Italian oratorio-opera affairs must now be added the cantata. Here the situation becomes quite complicated. That is, it is rather complicated for us; but for the seventeenth- and eighteenth-century poet it must not have been. He must have known before he put pen to paper what he was writing, what he had been asked to write, for what occasion, for what place. One certainly finds the terms opera, oratorio and cantata used with assurance and familiarity. In each case it meant something specific, and we must try to realize what this was and to what each genre entailed at the time. It is the only way we can hope to arrive at a better understanding of the histories of opera, of oratorio and of cantata.[17]

Though the term is commonly found applied in manuscripts of this period applied to solo vocal works, scholars have continued to refer to solo works with the title "serenata" as cantatas, effectively dismissing the given designation on the title page. Following the logic of the above quotation of Gianturco, it would seem that to Scarlatti, and many other composers of the period, or at the very least, to their scribes, a point was to be made when giving a solo cantata the additional title "serenata." In many manuscripts solo serenatas are surrounded by other works headed "cantata."[18]

Poets and Patrons

It was not only the composers who maintained the generic difference. The importance of poets in classifying the genre of a work has again been emphasized by Gianturco.[19] In an earlier, jointly authored article with Gabriella Biagi Ravenni, we read:

> [T]he seventeenth- and eighteenth-century poet knew exactly which poetic-musical genre he was writing, and if it were a madrigal, motet or canzone, an opera, oratorio or cantata he would have adjusted the subject accordingly.... [O]ne's choice is immediately limited to the contemporary dramatic genres of opera, oratorio and cantata.[20]

In the collection *Cantate per musica a voce sola di Francesco Maria Paglia* (I-Rvat, Vat. lat. 10204), there are seventy-two cantata texts, some designated for specific composers. The text of one Scarlatti solo serenata, *Sotto l'ombra d'un faggio*, is contained therein. Three other texts are also given the title "serenata" by Paglia: (1) *Ombre negre, ed oscure*, designated for Alessandro Melani; (2) *Là dove al sonno in braccio*, designated for Alessandro Scarlatti; and (3) *Taceva il mondo*, without designation. No musical source for *Là dove al sonno in braccio* has survived, and so it is not included in Hanley's thematic catalogue, but is given in the list of works of Scarlatti in the *New Grove*.[21] The fact that these serenata texts are found next to cantata texts, but with the serenata designation given specifically, would imply that they were conceived as serenatas before they were given to the composer, and that perhaps there is something in their textual genesis that marks them as serenatas rather than cantatas. It could not have been just a slip of the pen by poet, composer, or scribe.

This idea is further enforced by the poetry collection of Antonio Ottoboni, father of Pietro, one of Alessandro Scarlatti's most significant patrons. In an article on the music and poetry of Antonio Ottoboni, when discussing those poems he wrote to be set for two or more voices, Talbot and Colin Timms begin:

> Following the usage of Ottoboni's age, we would term items 8–11 "serenatas" if the poet had not reserved this word for certain solo cantatas (items 90, 109, 187, 227, 228 and 242) styled as traditional lovers' serenades.[22]

Again, confusion remains regarding these solo serenatas.[23] Though the poet entitled solo works as serenatas, for clarity, two subcategories of serenata are not allowed to co-exist by many modern scholars. According to them, the existence of serenatas for more than one voice seems to necessitate the expulsion of the solo variety from the genre. In the same way, and from the same article cited above, Gianturco and Biagi Ravenni conclude that the solo serenata is actually a cantata:

> As recent research has indicated, when cantatas were composed for definite occasions when they were intended to be performed not as intimate chamber music but publicly, in the afternoon or evening, and when more singers and instruments than just solo voice and continuo were employed ... they were that type of cantata called "serenata."[24]

Lastly, concerning the textual genesis of a work, one must not disregard the influence of the patron. Since music flourished under the auspices of regal and aristocratic patrons in this period, it is important to be aware of their role:

> It must not be concluded ... that it was only the poet who made decisions which had musical consequences; the patron certainly had his say, at least in deciding on the performers (which may mean that even the poet had to comply with the number of actor-singers to be involved in his cantata) and the location of the performance.[25]

In the case of a serenata, where the text is connected to an event of familial importance, such as a wedding, birth, or name day (or indeed a work such as an oratorical serenata with political overtones), the patron would have even more reason to dictate, or at least influence, textual content. As is clearly evident from journalistic sources, the composer was often the last to be mentioned.[26] In newspaper coverage of the day, much print space was given to the decorations and festivities, the patron being duly recognized, then sometimes the poet, and perhaps the composer, but not invariably. This is understandable when one keeps in mind the fact that the person writing was probably not a musician and thus apt to be much more influenced by the visual aspect of the performance. From the aural perspective, a non-musician's first point of reference for such a work is not the music, but the text, and therefore to such a person the poet is next in line of recognition. Often the singers were named while the composer remained in obscurity. It is harder to explain, from a modern-day point of view, why manuscripts sometimes bear the patron's name but not that of the composer.[27] However, this tendency reveals the relative position of the composer in society of that time.

An Occasional Work

One reason for giving a solo cantata the title serenata could be that it was composed for a specific occasion.[28] The title page of Alessandro Stradella's *Infinite son le pene* is designated by the composer "Cantata a 3 con gli istromenti di Soprano, Tenore e Basso, fatta per Serenata."[29] The closing phrase shows the functionality embedded in the term "serenata." Hanley identifies three cantatas of Scarlatti's oeuvre with specific references to events or locations: H. 27, *Al seren di si bel giorno;* H. 591, *Quando l'umide ninfe;*[30] and H. 606, *Quel pastor si gentil*. He gives the following five cantatas with probable occasional references: H. 362, *Là nel bel sen della regal Sirena;* H. 465, *No, non lasciar, canora e bella;* H. 581, *Qual bellezza divina?;* H. 738, *Tu mi lasciasti, o bella;* and H. 743, *Tu sei quella che al nome.*[31] It is interesting to note that none of the works identified by the serenata title given in manuscripts overlaps with this list, reinforcing the possibility that works included on the cantata list may have in fact been conceived as serenatas. As Hanley points out, the *Gazzetta di Napoli* and *Avvisi di Roma*, such rich sources of information on grand serenata occasions, reveal very little on the performance of solo cantatas.[32] Therefore, the lack of information regarding smaller serenatas should not necessarily be taken as evidence of their non-existence. Because of this lack of information concerning such private functions, it is more difficult to identify smaller serenatas.

There are however some references to solo works that could very probably have been serenatas. For example, in 1696, on 6 November the *Gazzetta di Napoli* relates a performance that took place two days earlier:

> Finally, the men of letters of this most faithful city also wished to contribute with their erudition to the happiness shared by all at the recovery of such a monarch. Thus they held a most noble assembly with the name of Accademia Napolitana . . . which was celebrated on Sunday evening the fourth of this month in the so-called great hall of the Viceroys in the Royal Palace. . . . The academicians were of various sorts, there being about sixty prelates, royal ministers, cavaliers, and jurists invited and called in alphabetical order of their names to recite their various Greek, Latin, Spanish, and Italian compositions in praise of His Majesty as well as of His Excellency. At the beginning a most pleasant cantata for solo voice by the renowned and famous contralto called "il Cortona" moved everyone to an elevated state, it being repeated with different words at the end after the oration.[33]

The description of the celebration in its entirety is reproduced in order to show that the celebration took the form of an encomium and therefore was in keeping with the tone of a serenata. The solemnity of the occasion is of course a result of the status of the celebrated person, Charles II of Spain. Thus, the concept of a serenata often encompasses a multifaceted festival, not only the music.[34] We have evidence here that a work for one voice[35] was felt appropriate to the above occasion, probably due to the fame of the performer. The usual grandeur and opulence shown during such an occasion by a multitude of performers was probably fulfilled by the famous castrato, Domenico Cecchi, known as "il Cortona."

At least one other record in the *Gazzetta di Napoli* seems to allude to solo performance and specifically to a solo serenata. It is from Naples, recorded on 17 September 1709:

> And on the same Sunday solemnizing the Commemoration of the Most Holy Virgin of Sorrows in all the churches and servants; in that of Santa Maria d'Ogni Bene from the same order, where there was an extremely ornate apparatus, with magnificent sacrifice, and first-rate music made possible by the devotion of the Duke of Madaloni, who gave a horse-drawn carriage to the renowned musician Matteo Sassano, from which he sang.[36]

Once again, the fame associated with this particular singer is the likely reason why it was recorded. Whereas the mentioning of the number of singers and musicians was normally a sign of the opulence expended on such an occasion, the appearance of Matteo Sassano[37] was already indication enough of the great expense paid by the patron.

Another source of information on serenatas is the libretti. Many of these survive, more than the manuscripts themselves, because very often they were printed and distributed to the audience. This was also the case with operas of the day. The serenata *Il Genio Austriaco: Il Sole, Flora, Zeffiro, Partenope e Sebeto* was given on 28 August 1713 in honor of the Empress Elisabeth's birthday. A copy of the libretto is extant in the Biblioteca Nazionale in Naples.[38] It gives the poet as Giuseppe Papis and the composer as Alessandro Scarlatti. It was clearly a grand occasion, with eighty instrumentalists and six choirs, but the music has been lost.[39] Griffin describes the format of the libretto:

> The libretto clearly shows that the serenata was divided into two parts. At the beginning of each part the Cavaliere Nicola Grimaldi representing IL GENIO AUSTRIACO sang a cantata as an introduction.[40]

Firstly, this shows that a solo cantata could be included in a serenata performance, thus making the solo serenata a subcategory recognized in its own time. Secondly, the fact that a person was representing someone else opens up the question of whether serenatas were acted, whereas current scholarship on the genre assumes that they were not.

Account books provide an additional source for records of performances, though even these do not seem to provide full records of all the performances that took place. Griffin notes that, despite the fact that Francesco Maria Ruspoli is reported to have presented several serenatas during the summer of 1706, the Marchese's account books for that period make reference to only a single work for solo voice:

> Pag. a di per rimborso di spese per regalo di Mad.a Carò per riceveta—2.88
>
> P.o Agosto 1706 Spese per regolare Madama Carò cantarina per ordine dell'Ill.mo Sig.re March. Padrone . . . di 31 Agosto 1706 Dom o Fattori
>
> Pag a Pro Castrucci disse d'ord: di V.a Ill.m Per dare alli due violini che sonorno la cantata come per ricevuta—2
>
> Il infra scritto ò ricev'to dal Sig.re Angelo Valeri scudi due moneta e sono per i due Violini della serenata del Ill.mo Sig.re M. Ruspoli questo 30 agosto 1706 Io Pietro Castrucci.[41]

Griffin concludes that these bills are for gifts to the singer Madama Carò and for the hiring of two violinists "in the performance of a cantata or serenata. In all likelihood this was the work for solo voice sung by Madama Carò."[42] Because Griffin earlier in his dissertation takes the position that a serenata is for two or more voices, he does not identify this solo performance by Madama Caro as a serenata.

One could assume that solo serenatas were still written for a specific person or occasion, perhaps a more private event. Whereas the *Gazzetta di Napoli* and *Avvisi di Roma* report the performance of large serenatas, particularly associated with political and regal events, it is understandable that smaller occasions would be less likely to be mentioned in such newspapers. Historians have commented that notices in these public sources are subject to the conditions similar to those applicable to today's media, that is, they were influenced by those with power seeking publicity for professional or political reasons.[43] However, a private diarist is less bound to reflect such influence, even though the entries themselves may be regarded as subjective. For example, Arnaldo Morelli's article is concerned with musical references found in the *Ephemerides cartariae* held in the Cartari-Febei archive in Rome. *Ephemerides cartariae* is a journal kept from 1642 through 1691 by Carlo Cartari, a member of the middle class. This source gives a view of daily cultural life in Rome, without the political slant shown by the public media. Within this source, one finds many descriptions of serenata festivities, as well as events of less public significance. For example, the following wedding celebration is recorded:

> 9 April 1671: Festivities celebrating the nuptials of a niece of Cardinal Altieri and the Duke Orsini of Gravina. In the evening the bride and groom were brought to the Altieri palace, where until three o'clock in the morning, with many ladies and gentlemen, etc., there was singing and playing, and they had a lavish supper of preserves and candies.[44]

It is at such an occasion that solo serenatas were likely to be performed. More specifically, a solo cantata is mentioned within the following account of serenata festivities:

> 21 April 1687: The same evening Abbot Elpidio Benedetti gave a festival performance for the recovery of the king of France by erecting an ornate facade to his own dwelling with pictures, coat of arms, and other ornaments with the portrait of the king, different kinds of torches and lamps, etc., and with continual playing, in turns, of exquisite trumpets and drums, many fireworks, and with the plentiful attendance of nobility and people. Adding to the festivities a cantata in praise of the king, which was printed and distributed, was sung by an expert female singer. Also distributed was a sheet with the engraving of the facade.[45]

The evening's entertainment described above certainly exhibits elements usually attributed to a serenata performance: elaborate decoration, the use of torches and other illumination, the use of trumpets and drums associated with outdoor music, song, and distribution of a printed text. Once again, the concept of serenata did not encompass only the music, but the festivities as a whole. An interesting observation is that Morelli, in the discussion that precedes the listing of documents from the *Catari-Febei* archive, refers to this festival above as a serenata:

> Again for the recovery of the French sovereign we have notice of a "francophile" serenata (but not in front of the church of the Trinità dei Monti) the following year: it was organized by the Abbot Elipidio Benedetti, attaché of the king of France in Rome, in front of his villa outside the San Pancrazio gate, and was concluded with a serenata performed by an "expert female singer."[46]

Aside from newspapers and diaries, another source of data on performance practice of serenatas is letters. One such source, documented by Paola Besutti, contains extracts of musical significance from a collection of letters, a result of an exchange between Carlo II Gonzaga di Nevers, the duke of Mantova from 1647 to 1665, via his secretary of state, Angelo Tarachia, and his ambassador in Rome, Abbot Francesco Tinti. The correspondence covers the period from 1655 to 1661. A musical connoisseur who was unhappy with local offerings, the duke sought music from prestigious Rome. Besutti extracts information on the production and transmission of Roman cantatas from this correspondence. The intense interest in the genre is not surprising, and it must be noted that among the numerous references to the cantatas exchanged there are in fact two instances of serenatas: (1) *Più non dorma il mio bene,* mentioned in two letters of 3 and 10 June 1656;[47] and (2) an untitled serenata by Giovanni Bicilli (1623–1705, *maestro di cappella,* Chiesa Nuova, S. Maria in Vallicella).[48] From the context of the correspondence it is evident that these works are for solo voice, especially the second example, which is also interesting from another point of view: the correspondence indicates that the work was "adjusted" to suit the baritone voice of this patron.[49]

Common Features of Solo Serenatas

It could be that the only difference between a solo serenata and a solo cantata is that the former is written specifically for a celebratory purpose. However, given the frequency of the usage of the title in the context of works for solo voice, it is worth inquiring what distinctive features these pieces have in common from a musical and textual point of view. It is time to explore further what the term serenata might have meant to musicians of the period, when applied to this solo genre.

Obbligato Instruments

The presence of obbligato lines, not only to play ritornelli between strophes of arias but also as an integral part of the aria textures, is a recurring feature already from the Neapolitan serenatas of the 1670s.[50] This is equally true of the serenatas of Alessandro Scarlatti, including some instances of recitativo accompagnato, such as the opening of *Notte, ch'in carro d'ombre.* Of the nine definitive serenatas by Scarlatti (as the authorship of a tenth, *Era l'oscura notte,* is questioned in this edition), two are accompanied by basso continuo only and are therefore rejected by Griffin from consideration as serenatas.[51] The frequency of two obbligato parts in the solo serenatas of Scarlatti is in stark contrast to his cantatas: of Scarlatti's output of more than seven hundred cantatas, more than 90 percent are for soprano and basso continuo alone.[52] The reason for the predominance of scoring for two instrumental obbligato lines may be related to outdoor performance, an oft-cited feature of serenatas. The addition of instruments may be regarded as not only an allusion to the origins of the genre (the amorous serenata played by wandering minstrels under a lady's balcony), but also as an aid to any acoustical problems created by the venue. The use of portable plucked instruments such as archlute and baroque guitar was for the same reason almost certainly to be regarded as an essential—if unspecified—part of the instrumental group for a serenata. The addition of instruments could focus the listener on the performance, as is the case when the orchestration of a work changes from voice and continuo to the sonority of an instrumental ensemble. The occasional nature of the serenata, and its status as a special event, could equally have provided the opportunity for Scarlatti to devise integrated vocal and instrumental structures that one may imagine to have required more intense rehearsal than those in which basso continuo aria with instrumental ritornello predominate.

"Hor che" Incipit and Textual Imagery

The Petrarchan *hor che* incipit was directly related to Renaissance serenatas, derived from the popularity of Petrarch's sonnet 164, *Hor che 'l ciel et la terra e 'l vento tace* (Now that the heaven and the earth and the wind are silent).[53] Of Scarlatti's solo serenatas, three begin with these words: H. 33, *All'hor che stanco il sole*; H. 511, *Hor che di Febo ascosi*; and H. 516, *Hor che l'aurato nume*. Considering this is a genre linked to a specific time of day and location, this descriptive setting of the scene is an intrinsic response built into the opening line of text.

Griffin comments correctly that none of the larger-scale serenatas begins in this fashion.[54] One of them, however, begins in a paraphrase of this opening: the dramatic serenata *Clori, Lidia e Filli* begins with the following text: "Già compito il suo giro vassi à tuffar nell'onde il bionde Nume" (Already having completed its rotation, the fair god [the sun] is going to dive into the waves). Particularly in the dramatic serenatas, this literary device is sometimes found at a conspicuous moment in the midst of the text. In *Venere e Adone,* it occurs in the recitatives "Pria che dal vago Oriente" and "Venere assai ti deggio."[55] It is a recurring device in *Amore e Virtù*, where Amore sings it three times in the first part, including (a) the opening, (b) a middle, and (c) closing recitatives:

(a) Ora che in me risplende face mortal . . .[56]
Now that the mortal torch shines in me . . .

(b) Or che di te l'istesso amor s'infiamma . . .[57]
Now that the same love inflames you . . .

(c) Or ch'un puro e casto ardore
è la fiamma ch'accende il sen d'amore . . .[58]
Now that a pure and chaste desire
is the flame that lights the bosom of love . . .

In the usual use of the literary formula, it is the sun that sets. Now, instead of the sun, it is Amore that is ablaze.

The *hor che* formula is most prominent in the oratorical serenata *Al fragor di lieta tromba*, as the final aria of Amore, and the conclusion of the debate:

Or che l'Ibero, or che 'l Danubio, e 'l Reno
Del Gran Carlo a le piante
Tributario sen' corre;
& or che 'l mira
Cinto di doppia Clamide la fronte,
Da lui sol brama Pace,
E dal suo braccio solo
De la tranquillità spera 'l consuolo.

Now that the Iberian, now that the Danube and the Rhine flow in tribute
to the feet of the Great Carlo,
and now that they gaze upon him
girded with a double breast plate,
from him alone seek Peace,
and from his authority alone
hope for the comfort of tranquility.[59]

In another extant oratorical serenata, again for Carlo VI, Holy Roman Emperor, *Partenope, Teti, Nettuno, Proteo e Glauco*, the bass character Glauco sings in his final aria as a conclusion to the debate, with the customary *hor che* formula: "Tremi il mondo paventi l'inferno or che sorgono a schiere dal'onde i guerrieri tremendi a pugnar" (The world should tremble, hell be fearful, now that the tremendous warriors arise from the waves to fight). It is a none-too-subtle reference to the might of the reigning power. The work ends with a triumphant chorus, joined by the soloists, and accompanied by a large orchestra.

Connections between Scarlatti's cantatas evoking the silent, terrifying-yet-consoling night and those found in Ovid's poetry have also been discussed.[60] In his discussion of Renaissance poetry in the book *The Light in Troy*, Thomas M. Greene traces Petrarch's opening of sonnet 164 to the classical topos of evocation of nightfall:

Hor che 'l ciel et la terra e 'l vento tace,
E le fere e gli augelli il sonno affrena,
Notte il carro stellato in giro mena
E nel suo letto il mar senz'onda giace . . .

Now that the heavens and the earth and the wind are
    silent,
and sleep reigns in the beasts and the birds,
night drives her starry car about,
and in its bed the sea lies without a wave . . .[61]

The incipit serves the purpose of setting the scene, a passage describing the calm stillness of the night and nature in general, giving the feeling of the prolongation of time throughout the use of the continuous present tense. This reflects the Virgilian opening to book 4 of the *Aeneid*, "Nox erat, et placidum carpebant fessa soporem corpora per terras, siluaeque et saeua quierant aequora" (It was night time, and throughout the lands tired bodies were resting, and the forests and harsh sea were at rest [4:522–24])—continuous duration is suggested by the use of the imperfect tense. Petrarch interrupts his Virgilian scene with its slow moving rhythmic flow, with the bold present tense verbs in the first person *vegghio, penso, ardo, piango* (I wake, I think, I burn, I cry), suddenly quickening the rhythmic pace. This sudden turn reflects the passage that immediately follows Virgil's scene setting, namely Dido's lengthy monologue, beginning "En quid ago? rursusne procos irrisa priores experiar?" (Alas, what am I to do? Shall I, though spurned, again approach my former suitor [i.e., Aeneas]? [4:535–35]).

This scene of tranquility is juxtaposed with anxiety of the scorned Dido; likewise the scene of Petrarch is broken by personal anguish. This oxymoronic tension is reflected with staccato effect by Petrarch with the opposites *dolce/pena, guerra/pace, dolce/amaro, risana/punge, martir/salute, moro/nasco*. The tranquil opening, sudden change in rhythmic flow, particularly through interrupting recitatives, using direct speech in the first person (see first person address below), together with rhetorical artifice—

oxymoron in particular—are a common flow of action in the texts of many seventeenth-century cantatas, the solo serenata type especially.

Many of these serenatas share other common imagery in their texts. While reference to the sun is frequent, whether it be a sunrise or sunset, at the beginning or end of a serenata,[62] it is nighttime, or at least evening, that is the usual setting for the sentiment expressed in these serenatas, as Mattheson says in his definition quoted above. Often in these solo serenatas the night was a desired place, where a forlorn lover could vent his frustrations in solitude.[63]

Sleep, obviously linked with the night, also occurs frequently. In one particular case, the music even had the intended function of putting the patron to sleep.[64] Further examples of the sleep motif outside the oeuvre of Scarlatti include Barbara Strozzi's serenata *Hor che Apollo è a Theti in Seno,* in which the beloved is induced to sleep by the night; and George Frideric Handel's *Nel dolce del oblio,* a cantata which, with the presence of the recorder obbligato line and the nighttime setting with sleeping lover, could arguably have been performed as a solo serenata. Performances of solo serenatas, alongside those specifically named cantatas, are documented by Owen Jander for the Duke Francesco II d'Este and his *Accademia de' Dissonanti* at Modena.[65] Reference to *dolce sonno* (sweet sleep) in one work, honorific references to the duke, together with instrumental clues, such as the presence of a trumpet and the use of concerto grosso/ripieno effects, mark these as typical examples of the solo serenata subcategory.

Allusions to water are common and very often provided a setting for the serenata performance.[66] It seems that the poet made use of the physical setting of the serenata in the text, thereby possibly linking the serenata to its performance location. The use of a compound meter, together with lilting, slurred articulations, illustrates musically the lapping of waves. Such features are common in connection with sea imagery. In the serenatas of the generation before Scarlatti, the incipit line frequently contains references to the marine setting of the performance at dusk, such as *Hor che nel Mar d'Atalante cadde naufrago il Sole,* a work by Giovanni Bonaventura Viviani (I-Nc 33.4.4, fols. 24r–29r). Marine references may feature throughout the text, even when the first line does not name the setting. Specific allusions to place may occur in the incipit line, particularly to Posilippo, the aquatic setting for many serenatas performed in Naples, such as *Di Pausilippo in sù l'herbosa sponda* by Antonio Farina (I-Nc 33.4.4, fols. 32r–40v).

Torches ("faci ardente") are often mentioned, as well as images of burning flames. Again, this may be linked to the performance venue, as torches were a frequent decoration of the outdoor nighttime event. Even in the academies, no expense was spared in the preparation of elaborate candles, as can be seen from the accounts of patrons, for example those of Ottoboni, held now in the *Archivio segreto* in the Vatican. The burning torch reveals a further connection to Petrarchan erotic imagery, as in *vegghio, penso, ardo, piango.*

Love Faithful or Unrequited

The protagonist in the serenata text is often the forlorn lover, distraught by an imminent departure. She or he professes undying love, with musical imagery, such as the ostinato bass line, symbolizing the lover's constancy and undying and often unrequited love.[67] Another scenario is the scorned lover, wasting away as a result of his treatment by the cruel lady. In this case, the protagonist often ends the work by seeking death, e.g., in *Hor che l'aurato nume.* It may at first strike one as odd that the serenata, which is by definition a celebratory piece, may have had such an emotive element. In order to address this supposed anomaly, let us turn back to the article by Freitas concerning the reception of the seventeenth-century cantata, so as to see how such a text might be received by its audience.

Freitas first refers to the negative way that seicento cantata poetry has been regarded by scholars in the nineteenth and twentieth centuries "as insincere and unoriginal," and by Prunières in particular, who refers to "the weakness, the bombast, and the bad taste of the words." Freitas sets out to re-evaluate seicento poetry from the point of view of its intent:

> [B]ecause . . . seicento cantatas were created and experienced within an environment that valued wit and ingenuity over emotional revelation, the modern notion of sincerity is largely irrelevant to historical criticism. Rather, contemporaries more likely experienced cantatas—both textually and musically—as convivial exhibitions of rhetorical skill than as the personal disclosures of the poet, composer or performer.[68]

Freitas bases his interpretation of these bourgeois gatherings on contemporary treatises on behavior game books, and contemporary accounts.[69] From Guazzo's *La civil conversazione* (first published in 1574, but due to its popularity reprinted several times during the seventeenth and eighteenth centuries all over Europe in several languages) an example is given where a gentleman is challenged to improvise a love lament addressed to one of the ladies present. His poem, strikingly similar to cantata poetry, centers on and ends with his approaching death from the sufferings of love. The audience, rather than being moved to tears at the sentiment, burst into laughter. It was not the "vicarious experience of emotion" that the audience sought, but amusement through, "like any other game, . . . a foundation for verbal display."[70]

And so, when examining the texts of these solo serenatas, intended for a discerning seventeenth- or eighteenth-century audience, one should assess the poetry on the grounds of the cleverness of its rhetoric and conceits, and how the composer then goes about setting this aspect of the poetry in music. The forlorn and/or faithful lover before the audience would probably not be greeted exclusively by sympathetic tears but by smiles at the wit of his address.

First Person Address

Colin Timms classifies the solo cantatas of Vivaldi by means of the nature of address. He examines the texts in order to determine whether the work is historic or non-historic. He explores the extent to which the cantata consists of lyrical or dramatic elements, particularly in respect to the use of dialogue, first-person (direct address), or third-person (narrative) forms.[71] All of the serenatas in this edition are in the first person, the performer directly addressing his or her audience. This could be related to the oratorical serenata delivery, where the characters, instead of being involved in a dramatic plot, present their side of a debate directly to the audience. In the case of a solo serenata, the performer presents his or her monologue to the audience, without means of a narrator.[72]

Closure

Often these serenatas end with the singer "dying away" on a long sustained note. For example, H. 710, *Sventurati miei penzieri*, ends in this way with the singer repeating the phrase "morir mi conviene" (to die suits me best) and fading away on a long sustained note, while the ostinato bass line continues its round. This is a very early work,[73] and this convention seems to be one that occurs more frequently in Scarlatti's earlier compositions, or at any rate in his works of the seventeenth century. Perhaps this style of fade-away ending is a compositional precursor to another even more remarkable type, the unaccompanied vocal exit, commonly heard in Scarlatti's dramatic serenatas.[74] Equally characteristic of Farina's and Viviani's serenatas is the vocal ending on the lowest note of the piece.[75]

The presence of the fade-away ending in both solo and dramatic serenatas may be seen as yet another example of exchange between the subcategories of serenata, and there are other cases in the cantata repertoire.[76] Also related are the duet cantatas, which of course lend themselves to dramatic dialogue. The duet cantatas H. 485, *O come bello con onde chiare*, and H. 19, *Ahi, che sarà di me?*, provide more examples of unaccompanied endings. Were these endings part of a serenata convention, with the vanishing singers leading smoothly to another part of the celebration, as dancing, fireworks, or refreshments?[77] Griffin says there are a few uncommon examples of such endings by other composers,[78] but these endings by Scarlatti are neither uncommon nor are there any indications of a da capo or ritornello to follow.

Notes

1. Edwin Hanley, "Alessandro Scarlatti's 'Cantate da Camera': A Bibliographical Study" (Ph.D. diss., Yale University, 1963), 13.

2. Griffin refers to them in "The Late Baroque Serenata in Rome and Naples: A Documentary Study with Emphasis on Alessandro Scarlatti" (Ph.D. diss., University of California, Los Angeles, 1983), 9, and in Alessandro Scarlatti, *Venere, Amore e Ragione: Serenata a 3*, ed. Judith L. Schwartz, with a historical introduction by Thomas E. Griffin, Recent Researches in the Music of the Baroque Era, vol. 104 (Madison: A-R Editions, 2000), xvii nn. 11 and 20. Hanley does not identify these works as serenatas in his dissertation, however. In chapter 2, "The Definition of the Repertory of Alessandro Scarlatti's Cantate da Camera" (pp. 65–66), he asserts that there are no stylistic differences between solo serenata and solo cantata, nor are there references to occasions. Like Strüver and Dent before him, he sees the solo serenatas as cantatas.

3. See Marie-Louise Catsalis, "The Serenata: A Movable Feast," in *Music Research: New Directions for a New Century*, ed. Michael Ewans, Rosalind Halton, and John A. Phillips (London: Cambridge Scholars Press, 2004), 15–26.

4. For documentary evidence on academies, see Arnaldo Morelli, "La musica a Roma nella seconda metà del Seicento attraverso l'archivio Cartari-Febei," in *La musica a Roma attraverso le fonti d'archivio, Atti del convegno internazionale, Roma 4–7 giugno 1992*, ed. Bianca Maria Antolini, Arnaldo Morelli, and Vera Vita Spagnuolo (Lucca: Libreria Musicale Italiana, 1994), entries 62 (academy of Queen Cristina), 74, 79, 81, and 82 (Accademia al Collegio Clementino); Thomas E. Griffin, *Musical References in the Gazzetta di Napoli, 1681–1725* (Berkeley: Fallen Leaf Press, 1993), entries 127 (l'Accademia di belle Lettere), 130 (Arcadi), 239 (Ottoboni), and 466 (Accademia di belle lettere, Collegio Clementino), among others. For bills and accounts associated with such gatherings, see Ursula Kirkendale, "The Ruspoli Documents on Handel," *Journal of the American Musicological Society* 20 (1967): 222–73, for the Ruspoli household; and Hans Joachim Marx, "Die Musik am Hofe Pietro Kardinal Ottobonis unter Arcangelo Corelli," *Analecta Musicologica* 5 (1968): 104–77, for the Ottoboni household, and "Die 'Giustificazioni della Casa Pamphilj' als musikgeschichtliche Quelle," *Studi musicali* 12 (1983): 121–87, for the Pamphilii household. For discussion on the *Accademie*, see Owen Jander, "The Cantata in Accademia: Music for the Accademia de' Dissonanti and their Duke, Francesco II d'Este," *Rivista italiana di musicologia* 10 (1975): 519–44; and Michael Talbot, "Musical Academies in Eighteenth-Century Venice," *Note d'Archivio*, nuova serie, vol. 2 (1984): 21–66. For the Accademia dell'Arcadia, founded in honor of Queen Christina of Sweden, of which Alessandro Scarlatti was a member, see Guido Chigi Saracini, *Gli Scarlatti: Raccolti in Occasione della Settimana Celebrativa (15–21 settembre 1940)* (Siena: Ticci, 1940); Roberto Pagano, *Scarlatti: Alessandro e Domenico, due vite in una* (Milan: Mondadori, 1985), 245–51; and Malcolm Boyd, "Rome: The Power of Patronage," in *The Late Baroque Era: From the 1680s to 1740*, ed. George J. Buelow, Music and Society (Englewood Cliffs, N.J.: Prentice Hall, 1993), 47–53.

5. Hanley, "Alessandro Scarlatti's 'Cantate da Camera,'" 10.

6. See Johann David Heinichen, *La Gara degli Dei* and *Diana su l'Elba*, ed. Michael Walter, Recent Researches in the Music of the Baroque Era, vols. 102 and 103 (Madison: A-R Editions, 2000); Scarlatti, *Venere, Amore e Ragione* (see note 2 above); and Alessandro Scarlatti, *Venere, Adone, et Amore: Original Version, Naples 1696 and Revised Version, Rome 1706*, ed. Rosalind Halton, RRMBE, vol. 157 (Middleton, Wis.: A-R Editions, 2009).

7. Antonio and Pietro Ottoboni and Ferdinando de' Medici, for example.

8. Roger Freitas, "Singing and Playing: The Italian Cantata and the Rage for Wit," *Music and Letters* 82 (2001): 510.

9. See Jander, "The Cantata in Accademia," 519–44; Lawrence Bennett, ed., The Italian Cantata in the Seventeenth Century, vol. 16 (New York and London: Garland, 1986), n.p.; and Freitas, "Singing and Playing," 515.

10. Griffin, historical introduction in Scarlatti, *Venere, Amore e Ragione*, xi.

11. Michael Talbot, "Vivaldi's Serenatas: Long Cantatas or Short Operas?" in *Antonio Vivaldi: Teatro musicale, cultura e società*, ed. Lorenzo Bianconi and Giovanni Morelli (Florence: Olschki, 1982), 70. The other two definitions concern the instrumental serenade from the classical period onwards, and the large-scale vocal serenata, a species of cantata.

12. Dinko Fabris, "La serenata a Napoli prima di Alessandro Scarlatti," in *La Serenata tra Seicento e Settecento: Musica, Poesia, Scenotecnica, Atti del convegno internazionale di studi, Reggio Calabria 16–17 maggio 2003*, ed. Nicolò Maccavino (Reggio Calabria: Laruffa Editore, 2007), 1:15–71.

13. The penchant for Italian vocal music, including the serenata, spread northwards over the Italian Alps throughout the Hapsburg empire. See the editions of Heinichen, *La Gara degli Dei* and *Diana su l'Elba*.

14. Taken from *Der vollkommene Capellmeister* (1739), ed. Margarete Reimann, Documenta Musicologica, vol. 5 (Kassel: Bärenreiter, 1954), 216–17; translation from Griffin, "The Late Baroque Serenata," 28.

> Unter den weltlichen Vocal-Sachen hat ausserhalb des Schau-Platzes billig den Vorzug Die Serenata a voce sola, oder Abend-Musik di piu Voci, sempre con Stromenti. . . .
>
> Der Serenaten Haupt-Eigenschafft muss allemahl die Zärtlichkeit, la tendresse, sein. Ich sage die Haupt-Eigenschafft: denn es gibt dieser Gattung noch sehr viele Neben-Umstände. Die Cantaten nehmen, jede für sich, allerhand Regungen und Leidenschafften an; doch nur eine zur Zeit, und stellen dieselbe auf eine historische Art, Erzehlungs-Weise, vor. Die Serenaten hergegen wollen alle mit einander vornehmlich von nichts anders, als von zärticher und starcker Liebe, als der Poet, bei denselben darnach richten, wenn er ihr rechtes Wesen treffen will. Es ist keine Melodie so klein, und kein Stuck so gross, ein gewisses Haupt-Abzeichen muss vor andern, und über andre darin herrschen, und sie von den übrigen deutlich unterscheiden: sonst heisst es wenig oder nichts.
>
> Es läufft demnach wieder die eigentliche Natur der Serenata, wenn man sich ihrer, so zu reden, ausser ihrem Element (ich meine den Affect) bei Glückwünschungen, öffentlichen Geprächen, beförderungen auf hohen Schulen u.s.w. bedienen will. Staats- und Regiments-Sachen sind ihr fremd: denn die Nacht ist keinem Dingen mit solcher innigen Freundschafft zugethan, als der Liebe und dem Schlaf. Jenen Händeln dienen die Oratorien und Aubaden oder Morgen-Musiken allerhand Art, und führen eine prächtige hochtrabende ermunternde Eigenschafft, in weltlichen Materien zum besondern Abzeichen, die sich zur Zärtlichkeit und geheimen Regung des Hertzens schlecht reimet. Derowegen haben auch die Oratorien mehr Stimmen nöthig; da es hergegen bei den Serenaten gar wol ein Solo, oder nur ein Paar Sänger bestellen können; welches ein abermahliges gut Abzeichen ist.

15. Griffin, "The Late Baroque Serenata," 31.

16. *The New Grove Dictionary of Music and Musicians*, 2nd ed. (hereafter NG2), s.v. "Mattheson, Johann" (p. 143), by George J. Buelow.

17. Carolyn Gianturco, "*Il Trionfo del Tempo e del Disinganno*: Four Case-Studies in Determining Italian Poetic-Musical Genres," *Journal of the Royal Musical Association* 119 (1994): 46.

18. One example among many outside the Scarlatti oeuvre is a collection of works by D. Simone Coya published in Milan in 1675. Its title page reads "L'AMANTE IMPAZZITO | con altre Cantate, e Serenate à solo, & à due con Violini | DEL SIG. | D. SIMONE COYA | Della Città Grauina del Regno di Napoli . . ." See T. M. Gialdroni, "Francesco Provenzale e la cantata a Napoli nella seconda metà del Seicento," in *La musica a Napoli durante il Seicento, Atti del convegno internazionale di studi, Napoli 11–14 aprile 1985*, ed. Domenico Antonio D'Alessandro and Agostino Ziino (Rome: Torre d'Orfeo, 1987), 131.

19. Carolyn Gianturco, "The Italian Seventeenth-Century Cantata: A Textual Approach," in *The Well-Enchanting Skill: Music, Poetry, and Drama in the Culture of the Renaissance, Essays in Honour of F. W. Sternfeld*, ed. John Caldwell, Edward Olleson, and Susan Wollenberg (Oxford and New York: Oxford University Press, 1990), 41–51.

20. Gabriella Biagi Ravenni and Carolyn Gianturco, "The Tasche of Lucca: 150 Years of Political Serenatas," *Proceedings of the Royal Musical Association* 111 (1984–85): 53.

21. NG2, s.v. "Scarlatti, Alessandro" (p. 391), work-list by Malcolm Boyd.

22. Michael Talbot and Colin Timms, "Music and the Poetry of Antonio Ottoboni (1646–1720)," in *Händel e gli Scarlatti a Roma, Atti del convegno internazionale di studi, Roma 1985*, ed. Nino Pirrotta and Agostino Ziino (Florence: Olschki, 1987), 380.

23. Although only the titles are given, together with information regarding the extant musical settings, the following observations can be made of a generical nature: item 90, *Elpino innamorato guardava un dì*, is set by Caldara with two violins as obbligato and addresses a love theme; item 109, *Hor che su letto algoso*, employs the Petrarchan incipit as well as using a sea theme ("letto algoso" means bed full of sea-weed); item 227 (and its revised version, item 228), *Spiegate pur, spiegate / Ombre notturne velo*, has a nocturnal setting. See below, "Common Features of Solo Serenatas."

24. Biagi Ravenni and Gianturco, "The Tasche of Lucca," 53–54.

25. Gianturco, "The Italian Seventeenth-Century Cantata," 51.

26. See Griffin, *Musical References in the Gazzetta di Napoli*, xxxi.

27. Hanley, "Alessandro Scarlatti's 'Cantate da Camera,' " 26.

28. The collection of autograph manuscripts held in Yale, described by Strohm as "Alessandro Scarlatti's Cantata Diary," indicate that some of these works were composed for specific occasions. See Reinhard Strohm, "Scarlattiana at Yale," in *Händel e gli Scarlatti a Roma*, 132–39.

29. Autograph manuscript, Venice, Biblioteca Nazionale Marciana It.IV.560, fols. 128r–141v.

30. The occasion referred to is the end of the vacation in Albano of Clement XI's nephew and his mother, and their imminent return to Rome, heralded in this work by a nymph from a neighboring lake; see Hanley, "Alessandro Scarlatti's 'Cantate da Camera,' " 65. The details of the occasional references in the other two works are not given.

31. Ibid., 9.

32. Ibid., 5.

33. "Finalmente hanno voluto altresi i Letterati, di questa Fedelis. Città; anch'essi contribuire colla loro virttù [sic] alle commune allegrezze per il riacquisto di un tanto Monarca. Onde formarono una nobilissima Assemblea col nome d'Accademia Napolitana . . . la quale Domenica sera 4. del corrente fù celebrata entro la gran Sala, detta de' Vicerè nel Real Palazzo. . . . Furono gli Accademici di varie qualità, essendovene stati Prelati, Regii Ministri, Cavalieri, e Giuristi fino al numero di 60. scritti, & altresi chiamati; per toglier le precedenze secondo l'ordine alfabetico de' loro nomi à recitar, sicome fecero le loro varie composizioni Greche, Latine, Spagnuole, & Italiane in lode della M.S. & anche di S.E. Dispose gli animi sul principio una gratissima cantata à solo, del rinomato, e celebre Contralto detto il Cortona, quale fu con altre parole replicata ancora finita, che fù l'Orazione." Quoted and translated in Griffin, "The Late Baroque Serenata," 258–59.

34. See Morelli, "La musica a Roma," 114 n. 23, and Stefanie Tcharos, "The Serenata in Early 18th-Century Rome: Sight, Sound, Ritual, and the Signification of Meaning," *Journal of Musicology* 23 (2006): 528–68.

35. In a subsequent entry of the *Gazzetta*, a correction is given: *Il Cortona* was actually a soprano. See Griffin, "The Late Baroque Serenata," 260.

36. "E nella stessa Domenica solennizzandosi la Commemorazione della Santissima vergine de' Dolori in tutte le Chiese de i Serviti; in quella di Santa Maria d'Ogni bene dello stess'Ordine, ov'era ricchissimo apparato, con sacra magnificenza, e scelta Musica fatta fare dalla divozione del Duca Madaloni, che regalò una Carozza con Cavalli al rinominato Musica Matteo Sassano, che vi cantò." Quoted in Griffin, *Musical References in the Gazzetta di Napoli,* 52 (document 219); translation by Catsalis.

37. Matteo Sassano is the most often mentioned singer in the surviving issues of the *Gazzetta di Napoli*, mentioned fifty-six times, outnumbering the most often mentioned composer, Alessandro Scarlatti, who is mentioned thirty-seven times; see Griffin, *Musical References in the Gazzetta di Napoli,* xxix–xxx.

38. Griffin, "The Late Baroque Serenata," 648.

39. The details of scoring are given on page 5 of the printed libretto (ibid., 651).

40. Ibid.

41. Ibid., 517–18.

42. Ibid.

43. See Morelli, "La musica a Roma," 108, and Griffin, *Musical References in the Gazzetta di Napoli,* xxiii.

44. "9 aprile 1671; festeggiamenti per la celebrazione del matrimonio di una nipote del cardinale Altieri con il duca Orsini di Gravina: La sera si portano gli sposi al palazzo de' sig.ri Altieri nel quale sino alle tre hore di notte, l'intervento di molte dame, cavalieri etc. fu sonato e cantato, et fatta lauta colatione di confetture e canditi." Quoted in Morelli, "La musica a Roma," 123 (document 21); translation by Catsalis.

45. "21 Aprile, 1687: La sera del medesimo il s.r abbate Elpidio Benedetti diede il compimento alle feste per la ricuperata del re <di francia> con havere ornata la facciata della propria habitatione con pitture, imprese ed altre vaghezze con il ritratto del re, torcie, facole, padelle etc., e con suoni continui a vicenda di trombetti esquisiti e tamburi, quantità di razzi a corda ed in alto, e con numeroso concorso di nobiltà e di popolo. Compì l'allegrezza una cantata fatta in lode del re da una cantarina esperta, distribuita in stampa. Come anche fu distribuito un foglio con l'intaglio della facciata." Quoted in ibid., 132 (document 64); translation by Catsalis.

46. "Sempre per la guarigione del sovrano francese abbiamo notizia di una serenata 'francofila' (ma non davanti la Trinità dei Monti) l'anno seguente: essa venne organizzata dall'abate Elpidio Benedetti, agente del re di Francia a Roma, davanti alla sua villa fuori porta San Pancrazio, e fu conclusa da una serenata eseguita da una 'cantarina esperta.'" Ibid., 116; translation by Catsalis.

47. Paola Besutti, "Produzione e trasmissione di cantate romane nel mezzo del Seicento," in *La musica a Roma attraverso le fonti d'archivio,* 156.

48. Ibid., 161. See also Roberto Pagano, *Alessandro and Domenico Scarlatti: Two Lives in One,* trans. Frederick Hammond (Hillsdale, N.Y.: Pendragon Press, 2006), 149.

49. Besutti, "Produzione e trasmissione di cantate romane," 161. Hanley has found many instances of Scarlatti cantatas in various transpositions (see "Alessandro Scarlatti's 'Cantate da Camera,'" 21–22).

50. See Fabris, "La serenata a Napoli prima di Alessandro Scarlatti," table 4 (pp. 32–35) and table 5 (pp. 37–40).

51. Griffin, "The Late Baroque Serenata," 9. Of the three cantatas listed by Hanley as having definite occasional references, only one is with obbligato instruments; of the five with possible occasional references, again only one is with instruments. See Hanley, "Alessandro Scarlatti's 'Cantate da Camera,'" 9.

52. *NG2*, s.v. "Scarlatti, Alessandro," section 10, "Cantatas" (p. 381), by Edwin Hanley.

53. Alessandro Stradella uses this type of incipit in three of his vocal works: the serenata *Il Damone* for seven soloists and instruments begins with "Hor che il mondo ristaura"; another serenata of the same name, for five soloists and instrumentalists, opens with "Hor che l'alme ristaura il ciel"; and the cantata for two soloists and instruments, *Or ch'alla dea notturna*. Of the four serenatas that are reproduced in the Luigi Rossi volume of the Garland series, The Italian Cantata in the Seventeenth Century (vol. 1, ed. Francesco Luisi), two begin in this way: *Hor ch'in notturna pace* and *Hor che notte guerriera d'ombre, d'horrori armata* (both are three voice serenatas). For Barbara Strozzi (vol. 5, ed. Ellen Rosand), one serenata is given: *Hor che Apollo è a Theti in Seno*. A solo serenata, it is one of the few works in which she includes obbligato violin lines. For Maurizio Cazzati (vol. 8, ed. Anne Schnoebelen), two solo serenatas are given: *Ombre secrete udite*, of which the first aria begins "Or che d'astri rilucenti richiamato è il Ciel seren"; and *Or ch'ascoso nell'onde il dio del lume*. For Alessandro Scarlatti (vol. 13, ed. Malcolm Boyd), cantata no. 14 is *Allor ch'il dio di Delo guida il carro infiammato in altro Cielo*, yet another metaphor for the setting sun. In the Wellesley Edition Cantata Index Series, fascicle 4 (ed. Owen Jander [Wellesley, Mass.: Music Department, Wellesley College, 1969]), devoted to the works of Stradella, in addition to the works already mentioned above, two are given: *Or che stanco dal corso a le sua Teti in sen Febo riposa* and *Ora ch'è il di già spento e all'esequie* (these have been attributed to Pollarollo). Fascicle 5 (ed. Gloria Rose, 1966), devoted to the works of Giacomo Carrissimi, contains *Hor che di sirio, alla gran face estiva* (text by Colonna). Fascicle 2 (ed. Irving Eisley, 1964), devoted to the works of Mario Savioni, contains *Hor che già stanco il sole ne suoi lunghi viaggi*.

54. Griffin, "The Late Baroque Serenata," 9.

55. Alessandro Scarlatti, *Il Giardino di Amore: Serenata für Sopran, Alt, Soloinstrumente, Streichorchester und Basso Continuo,* ed. Otto Drechsler (Frankfurt am Main: Hansen, 1963), 43 and 47, respectively.

56. Alessandro Scarlatti, *Amore e Virtù; ossia, Il trionfo della Virtù: Cantata a due voci con stromenti,* ed. Antonio Tirabassi (Brussels: Schott Frères, 1923), 4.

57. Ibid., 18.

58. Ibid., 29.

59. The manuscript is reproduced in facsimile in the Scarlatti volume of The Italian Cantata in the Seventeenth Century, vol. 13, ed. Malcolm Boyd, no. 25, pp. 187–222, and the libretto is also reproduced as an addendum; translation by Catsalis.

60. Rosalind Halton, "Night and Dreams: Text, Texture, and Night Themes in Cantatas by Alessandro Scarlatti," in *Music Research: New Directions for a New Century,* 29.

61. Translation from Thomas M. Greene, *The Light in Troy: Imitation and Discovery in Renaissance Poetry* (New Haven, Conn.: Yale University Press, 1982), 116.

62. See, e.g., the closing recitative of *Eurilla, amata Eurilla,* or the opening recitative of *All'hor che stanco il sole*. The imagery of the sun was common to the Medici festivals (see Alois Maria Nagler, *Theatre Festivals of the Medici, 1539–1637* [New Haven, Conn.: Yale University Press, 1964], 10, 23, 61) and may in fact suggest a dramatic edge to this genre, being related to the Aristotelian concept of a twenty-four-hour period for storytelling. Both Timms and Talbot pose the question of whether Vivaldi's cantatas were dramatic in conception and origin or not, that is, whether they are scenes from unwritten operas. See Colin Timms, "The Dramatic in Vivaldi's Cantatas," 97–129, and Talbot, "Vivaldi's Serenatas," 67–96, both in *Antonio Vivaldi*. Certainly these serenatas are like dramatic monologues, and it is difficult to conceive of performances of them without histrionic gestures of some kind.

63. See Halton, "Night and Dreams," 27–39. Of course, throughout *Notte, ch'in carro d'ombre,* "Night" is addressed as an allegorical figure.

64. Freitas, "Singing and Playing," 514.

65. Jander, "The Cantata in Accademia."

66. For instance, the location of the bank of a river is the setting of *Sotto l'ombra d'un faggio,* and in *Hor che l'aurato nume,* the aria "Alle sponde dell'onde di Lethe" employs the compound

rhythm associated with the undulation of the waves. Given that performances on the water of the dramatic serenata were common, it is feasible then to imagine that performances of these solo serenatas too may have been performed in marine settings, such as the bay of Mergellina, Naples.

67. See, e.g., the aria "Se taccio, se parlo" of *Sventurati miei penzieri*, or at the end of the final recitative of *All'hor che stanco il sole*, at the text "mora tra l'ombre un c'ha perduto il sole."

68. Freitas, "Singing and Playing," 510.

69. See ibid., 511 n. 12.

70. Ibid., 513.

71. See Timms, "The Dramatic in Vivaldi's Cantatas."

72. Two of the solo serenatas of Scarlatti, *All'hor che stanco il sole* and *Sotto l'ombra d'un faggio*, open with a short recitative in the third person, setting the scene as would a narrator, but both works adopt the use of the first person for all that follows.

73. See the critical report under "Sources," p. 155.

74. The fade-away ending is a feature of Scarlatti's music that is first noted by Edward J. Dent in *Alessandro Scarlatti: His Life and Works* (1905; 2nd ed. with additions by Frank Walker, London: Edward Arnold, 1960), 90–91, and discussed in Griffin, historical introduction in Scarlatti, *Venere, Amore e Ragione*, xv–xvi.

75. Examples from I-Nc 33.4.4 are *Riposa ò bella* (Farina, fols. 1r–12r), *Cintia, dolente e mesto alle tue mura* (Farina, fols. 13r–20v), and *Hor che nel Mar d'Atalante* (Viviani, fols. 24r–29r).

76. For example, in H. 606, *Quel pastore sì gentil*, the bass line drops out, perhaps leaving the voice alone, but because the violin parts to this cantata are lost one cannot be certain. The final lines, "Il pastor d'ogni pastore dice al ciel egli sarà" (The shepherd of all shepherds says to heaven he shall go) are reminiscent of the pastoral cantatas often performed at Christmas time, and the singer is asked to sing an ascending scale finishing at three Ds above middle C, thus ascending into the heavens. And H. 9, *A voi che l'accendeste*, is an example of a cantata for soprano and continuo only that has an unaccompanied ending. The poet of this cantata is Francesco Maria Paglia, librettist of a significant number of serenatas and operas by Scarlatti in the 1690s. I am indebted to Rosalind Halton for bringing this cantata to my attention.

77. See Nicolò Maccavino, "La Serenata a Filli 'Tacete Aure Tacete' e le altre Serenate datate 1706 di Alessandro Scarlatti," in *La Serenata tra Seicento e Settecento*, 2:471.

78. Griffin, historical introduction in Scarlatti, *Venere, Amore e Ragione*, xv.

Musical Style and Performance

Rosalind Halton

The tradition of compositions for evening occasions that flourished in both Rome and Naples in the late seventeenth century provides the framework for the works by Alessandro Scarlatti presented here. Though we lack dates and specific occasions of composition, these works may be assumed to date from the 1680s to 1690s, with the exception of the final two works, *Notte, ch'in carro d'ombre* and *Hor che di Febo ascosi*, the second of which is said to have carried the date 1704 in a source destroyed in World War II.[1] These pieces entitled "Serenata" or "Serenata a voce sola" in at least one source give a fascinating insight into Scarlatti's relationship to the Neapolitan serenata tradition and the distinctive elements of structure and musical imagery that he brought to it.

Tonal Structure

Alessandro Scarlatti's expansion of tonal structure is among his most characteristic contributions to the cantata. The works in this volume encompass a style change from the cantata based around a single tonic to structures of contrasting arias—typically four—operating across a wide range of keys. The design of *Notte, ch'in carro d'ombre* illustrates the extreme contrasts of tonality envisaged by Scarlatti already by the early eighteenth century: from an instrumental introduction and accompanied recitative in F-sharp minor, the keys of the subsequent arias are D major, E minor, F minor, and F-sharp minor. Here the flat/sharp polarity, and the contrasts of expression and sonority, could hardly be more pronounced. Though less extreme in the juxtaposition of tonalities, the scheme of *Hor che di Febo ascosi* is almost as wide ranging: D major (instrumental introduction, opening recitative, and first aria), B-flat major (second aria), C minor (third aria), and D major (concluding aria)—key choices that are concentrated by the absence of da capo form in the final two arias.

The use of such contrasted flat and sharp tonalities within a single work marks a radical departure from the hexachord system that was still the familiar framework of the late-seventeenth-century composer. The natural hexachord—the modal structure of scales without a key signature—could include scales beginning on A or D (both with minor third), or on C, F, or G (with major third). The keys with one or more flat in the key signature had their basis in the soft hexachord, usually featuring minor third and minor sixth in the scale. In late-seventeenth-century Italy, D minor, G minor, and C minor (in modern terms) could all be signed with a key signature of one flat and modifying accidentals, indicated with varying degrees of exactness and always counting on the modal knowledge of the singer to supply missing accidentals. A key signature with one or more sharps indicated the hard hexachord, translating mainly to D major or A major from the modern musician's perspective, but potentially also keys such as B minor, F-sharp minor, and E major.

Though the hexachord system evolved as part of the technique of vocal polyphony, by the late seventeenth century aspects of instrumental timbre and tuning also played a part in determining the choice of key to evoke a particular emotional color. The bright sonority of violins in the sharp keys meant that their use was generally associated with strong and assertive emotional affect, and this implied a less delicate delivery in performance than pieces in flat keys, with their basis in the soft hexachord. The association of D major with trumpets and thus warfare contributed to this, an association so regularly observed by composers that when Scarlatti chooses D major for a soft piece—as in the first aria of *Notte, ch'in carro d'ombre*—it receives the special marking "adagio e piano."

According to the evolving usage of the hexachord system in Italy, an extended work for one singer and instruments might emphasize different points within its tonic and even contrasting inflections of major and minor, but it would usually retain its hexachordal identity as defined by the opening key signature and tonic. (The greater variety of opera key schemes is a factor that goes with the depiction of character contrasts, their opposing interests, and a broader time scale.) For example, the serenatas (largely for solo voice) of composers such as Antonio Farina (dates unknown), Giovanni Bonaventura Viviani (1638–after 1692), and Giovanni Cesare Netti (1649–86) found in Neapolitan manuscripts of the late seventeenth century[2] show extended structures within either the natural or soft hexachord, much less commonly the hard hexachord. A minor, D minor, and noticeably C minor are keys that predominate in this repertoire, with inflections in recitatives tending to move to the soft hexachord. Through the works in this volume, we see Scarlatti increasingly opening out the tonal and expressive structure to draw on both sharp and flat keys within a single work.

Serenata poetry typically portrays the outpourings of a solitary character to the night—thus the tone established by the opening music would set the atmosphere for the whole piece. Variety of metrical pattern, texture, and tempo figures regularly in the Neapolitan serenatas of the 1670s, but they do not display the type of tonal contrasts that were to become the hallmark of Scarlatti's solo serenata settings. Probably the earliest of the pieces entitled "Serenata a voce sola" attributed to Scarlatti is *Sventurati miei penzieri,* a work without da capo arias that revolves around a single tonic, with many permutations of meter, motif, and phrasing. Like Netti's solo serenata, *Nella notte più fosca,*[3] this work is set in C with minor third and key signature of one flat. It contains passages in both 3/2 and compound meter with dotted rhythm (6/8 in *Sventurati,* 12/8 in *Nella notte più fosca*). In both these C-minor works for soprano and basso continuo, the dotted compound section is based around G, but it is the 3/2 aria which predominates with two strophes and ends the work.

Though Scarlatti's writing here is closely parallel to examples by Netti and Viviani, some features of *Sventurati* create an individual flavor: the almost constant imitation between bass and vocal line, and the obsessive motivic repetition of the closing aria, "Se taccio, se parlo." Here the short-breathed phrases embody the hesitation of the "agonized" lover, and the choice of C minor enables the composer to use a wide vocal range (c' to a♭"), with phrase echoes placed in the lower octave that reinforce the lover's silence.

Whereas *Sventurati miei penzieri* contains no hint—other than the laments of the tormented lover—of a night setting, *Eurilla, amata Eurilla* has at least two textual indications to justify the term "serenata," which figures on the title page of at least two contemporary copies, both by the same copyist. These occur in the final recitative, at the text "ma già sorge l'Aurora" (but dawn is breaking already), and with the final "addio"—a farewell that also brings to an end the much larger-scale serenata *Hor che di Febo ascosi*. Just like *Sventurati miei penzieri, Eurilla, amata Eurilla* is based around one principal key, in this case B minor, but with an aria of two strophes forming the centerpiece in the subdominant key of E minor ("Lungi ancor dal petto amante"), thus preserving the hexachordal flavor of the whole. The style is similar to that of other seventeenth-century cantatas of Scarlatti in that recitative frequently turns to arioso through repetition of a text line (e.g., "lasciando mio cor" in the first recitative; "il nodo sciorre onde m'avvinse amore" in the second recitative; and "Vado a penar, vado a morir" in the final recitative). The two arias, composed of short motivic fragments, strike a more popular tone. Compared with the intensity of C minor in compositions on night subjects from the mid-seventeenth century,[4] it seems as if B minor does not have a fixed expressive profile, moving between an almost sacred arioso style and a more staccato delivery of text and phrase in the arias.

By far the most numerous examples of Neapolitan serenatas before Scarlatti are composed for solo voice and two violins,[5] which is the scoring of the remaining pieces in this volume. Two main sources of inspiration were available to the young Scarlatti: not only the Neapolitan serenatas but equally those of Alessandro Stradella (1639–82), which formed an important part of the musical environment in Rome in the 1670s. From Stradella's music came the opportunity to absorb a flexible approach to the relationship between recitative and ritornello aria, a varied tonal palette, and a lively interaction between voice and violins. In Scarlatti's solo serenatas we find many different treatments of the relationship between voice and violins. The introductory sinfonia of a serenata could be either concise, introducing the voice almost at once, as in *Prima d'esservi infedele*, or very extensive, as in *Perché tacete, regolati concenti?* A violin ritornello could introduce an aria, or enter after the aria, using the first motif of the voice or some later material. Arioso treatment of recitative continues to appear in the serenatas with violins, as well as passages in which the voice plays a part within a polyphonic string texture, for example the final movement of *Hor che l'aurato nume* with its imitative texture based on the vocal phrase "Ah! fiera sorte."[6]

For the most part, key schemes in Scarlatti's seventeenth-century serenatas for solo voice with violins are fixed around a tonic that retains its ascendancy for much of the work. Key contrasts are fixed within the orbit of the prevailing hexachord. Thus *All'hor che stanco il sole* is in F major, with arias in D minor and B-flat. *Hor che l'aurato nume* is in C minor, with arias in G minor, B-flat, and E-flat. *Perché tacete, regolati concenti?* is in D minor (or, in the transposed version discussed in the critical report, in C minor), with arias in F major and G minor. Tempo and meter contrasts play an important part in these works—most notably in *Hor che l'aurato nume*, whose arias are juxtaposed without intervening recitatives until the penultimate section of text, "Sì, sì, fuggi cor mio," prompts a recitative setting with indicated Presto and Adagio contrasts.

The most remarkable work within this group is *Prima d'esservi infedele*, which uses the unifying feature of a recapitulation of the very opening motif as the conclusion of the whole work. From the "neutrality" of the natural hexachord (Dorian mode, D minor), Scarlatti moves first to F major for the strophic aria "Quando sorge l'aurora" and then to an aria based around A minor, "Se la sorte avesse in seno." This latter is neither strophic nor da capo in form and concludes with a brief instrumental coda that grows out of the final vocal phrase, rather than recapitulating the opening music as a regular ritornello. Even more remarkably, each text line is set with its own melodic and rhythmic contour and accompanying texture, so that formally and tonally the aria can only be described as a through-composed form. As its textual extremes are the lines "il velen lambisci e mori" (you will lap up the poison and die) and "ma t'inganni, o cieca sorte" (but you delude yourself, O blind fate). For the first of these lines Scarlatti introduces the pitch D-flat into the vocal line, a change of direction reinforced by the A-flat triad on beat 1 of measure 20.[7] The prominent D-flat is eventually resolved as a Neapolitan inflection in C minor where the music cadences four measures later. A new episode in F major follows ("Tutta lieta all'hor direi" [Completely happy then I would say]), translated into laughing triplet figures. At the introduction of the line "ma t'inganni," Scarlatti introduces another semitone change, this time a' to a♯' in the vocal line, situating the music in B minor—as far to the hard hexachord as the "il velen" line had gone to the soft hexachord. Both excursions to flat and sharp sides are launched from the "natural" D minor/Dorian, which returns throughout this A-minor aria, as a reminder of the work's overall tonic. With *Prima d'esservi infedele* Scarlatti reaches a new level in the integration of formal, tonal, and textual aspects. The survival of several careful copies of the work suggests that it was highly valued by the composer and/or his patron.

Among Scarlatti's seventeenth-century serenatas the one that most openly acknowledges the style of Stradella is *All'hor che stanco il sole*. From the opening measures of the sinfonia to the meters and styles of the arias (3/2 with a vocal line moving smoothly in half and whole notes, 6/8 with dotted rhythms, common time with chromatic harmonies), and with the imperceptible transitions between recitative and arioso (for example, in mm. 14–22 of the first recitative), this work would evoke for contemporary listeners the sound world of the composer whose career had begun so promisingly in Rome under the patronage of Queen Christina, but who had subsequently met such a violent and untimely end.

It seems inevitable that the young Scarlatti would have absorbed the style and energy of the other "AS" and have sought to emulate his musical language.[8] Even the appearance of Stradella's most characteristic harmonies, such as the repeated subdominant preparation of the cadence in various inversions such as 6/4/3 and 6/5, has an unmistakable place in this work—first at the words "al susurrar de' venti" in the first recitative, taken up by the violins; and later in the 6/8 aria "S'alla bocca del caro" at the line "più d'un bacio." In this aria Scarlatti achieves the playful tone, lucid phrase construction, and ordering of harmonic progressions that he could have modelled on a work such as Stradella's "Serenata a due voci," *Or ch'alla dea notturna*.[9] The soprano "Aria con istromenti" of this work, "Cortesia gentilezza decora," could similarly be heard as a direct predecessor of Scarlatti's aria "Clori bella, e dove sei?" in its phrasing constructed through the constant interplay of short vocal and violin phrases. Having established the pattern, Scarlatti continues to devise arias in which the violin writing constantly echoes and amplifies the vocal line, from the bouncy triple "Deh, torna mia vita" (3/4) to the final lines of the work based on the vocal motif "mora tra l'ombre."

The only one of these works to survive only in a French source,[10] *Hor che l'aurato nume*, also appears to have the most unusual structure—a succession of arias unbroken by recitative, though substantial recitative passages are featured at both the opening and towards the close of the work. This time the tonic of C minor is pushed to the limits of flat-minor coloring, with the darkness of the text reflected in triads such as B-flat minor (at "Io, nemico di luce" in the first recitative). In the final aria, the accented vocal notes a♭' (m. 5) and d♭' (m. 13) at the beginning of the phrase "dammi la morte" are made all the more darkly prominent by being introduced by the much more open sounds of G minor and D minor. The F-minor triad inexorably leads to the plagal ending of the work, an example of the conclusion as death wish.

Such effects are not unprecedented in the Neapolitan serenata repertoire, some of which at least we may assume to have been known to Scarlatti. In the serenatas of Antonio Farina and Viviani (among the most prolific composers in the genre), the minor mode appears more regularly than the major, with A minor, D minor, and G minor the most commonly chosen for the tonic of a work. For the serenata *Eccomi ò Lilla ad ammollir col pianto*, Viviani chooses C minor,[11] and it may be no coincidence that the centerpiece of another night piece by Scarlatti, *Silenzio, aure volanti*, is a C-minor aria with violins on the text "Piangerò forse chi sà, avrà vanto il mio pianto d'ammollir sua crudeltà."[12] From Viviani's music Scarlatti could have been familiar with the use of B-flat minor and even E-flat minor triads in recitative, and arias in keys as far afield as F minor and A flat major.[13]

Sotto l'ombra d'un faggio, on the other hand, has only two tonal centers, with the two outer arias in E minor and the central aria in B-flat. The unexpected contrast—with the two principal keys separated by a tritone—places the work somehow between two worlds: that of the seventeenth-century serenata with its modally based repertoire of tonal relationships, and the eighteenth-century form of four recitatives and arias set in a scheme of both flat and sharp keys. The special flavor of such keys and modulations within the context of the work is a feature to be recognized in the performance of these works.

Aria Types

The da capo aria becomes predominant in Scarlatti's operas and cantatas already by the early 1690s; but in the works in this volume it is not yet the norm until the works clearly belonging to the first decade of the eighteenth century. This in itself indicates that the majority of these works come comparatively early in Scarlatti's career. An extraordinary diversity of aria types is seen in these works, originating in the composer's mastery of managing the dialogue between voice and violins. The intent to create continuity between recitative, arioso, and aria predominates. In many cases the strophic aria with ritornello is structured in an ABA design. Some have unexpectedly extended ritornello writing, for example, those of *All'hor che stanco il sole*. Through-composed arias with no element of recapitulation appear as late as *Hor che di Febo ascosi* (third and fourth arias), as well as in the seventeenth-century work *Prima d'esservi infedele*. Even in the da capo arias of *Notte, ch'in carro d'ombre*, the instrumental interludes are recomposed in a way that blurs the boundaries between the end of the B and return to the A sections, preserving the momentum of the music.

Recurrent Elements in Scarlatti's Solo Serenatas

The Sleep Aria

The evocation of sleep is one of the most common aria subjects in seventeenth-century serenatas. In Francesco Maria Paglia's collection *Cantate per musica a voce sola* (in I-Rvat, Vat. lat. 10204),[14] the poetic texts designated as "Serenata" regularly contain an aria on the subject of sleep—either a plea for sleep and dreams, or a declaration of resisting sleep. For instance, the serenata text *Ombre negre ed oscure* ("Musica di Alessandro Melani") has as second aria "Deh vegliate mie care pupille, / Non dormite ch'è troppa viltà . . ."; second strophe: "Sì dormite pupille adorate, / Non v'aprite ch'è troppa beltà . . ."[15] The unattributed serenata *Taceva il mondo, e sotto oscuro velo* (also from Ms. 10204) has as first aria "Tu dormi, ò mio bene / e sogni l'empietà. / Io veglio alle pene, / e penso fedeltà."; second strophe: "Tu dormi, e ferisce / lo sguardo tuo crudel. / Io veglio, e languisce / Il petto mio fedel."[16] And sleep arias feature regularly in the Neapolitan seventeenth-century serenatas. For example, Antonio Farina's serenata for soprano and two violins, *Cintia, dolente e mesto alle tue mura*,[17] has a sleep aria in G minor with imitative violin texture, based on the same metrical structure of Paglia's poem, with its short lines of six syllables introduced by an anacrusis and lending itself to a triple-meter setting: "Se dormi, ben mio / deh sogna d'amarmi."

The works in this volume include four arias that evoke sleep: "Dormi, ma sappi almen" of *Perché tacete, regolati concenti?*; "Io dormivo presso al rivo" of *Sotto l'ombra d'un faggio*; "Con l'idea d'un bel gioire" of *Notte, ch'in carro d'ombre*; and "Dormite, posate" of *Hor che di Febo ascosi*. Table 1 shows the variety of forms in these pieces as well as their features in common; most hypnotic is the F-minor "Con l'idea," while the through-composed "Dormite, posate" presents a unique sound picture with its constant eighth-note motion of the instrumental accompaniment from which the vocal line gradually emerges. A slow rate of harmonic change and a texture of simply voiced triadic harmony are the essential elements of Scarlatti's language in his sleep arias, often contrasting with the contrapuntal complexities of the surrounding music.[18]

Continuity between Ritornello and Aria

In the baroque opera repertoire the listener was used to hearing clearly marked contrasts between the formal boundaries of the da capo aria. Such perceptible separation seems to be at the opposite pole from Scarlatti's aim in both *Notte, ch'in carro d'ombre* and *Hor che di Febo ascosi*. Instead of an indication for exact repetition of the ritornello material, it is rewritten to produce an effect of continuity between B section and da capo, in some cases merging imperceptibly into the return of the A section. In the case of an aria inviting rest, such as "Vieni, o Notte" (first aria of *Notte, ch'in carro d'ombre*), the gently rocking motion of the music is at one with the overlapping of breaks between sections of text. This characteristic may have arisen from the continuity between formal elements in the seventeenth-century works. The merging of recitative into arioso, ritornello, and aria is one of the most conspicuous elements, often produced by introducing a text-line with an anticipating motif played by violins. Maybe the most subtle instance of structural overlap in these works is the seamless recapitulation of the opening vocal music in the final recitative of *Prima d'esservi infedele* (from m. 8). Here it is the voice that draws the violins into dialogue, rather than the opposite—as in the opening measures of the work—producing a moment of recall that parallels the self-quotation of the opening text line: "I will say: 'Before being unfaithful to you, beautiful eyes, I will die.'"

Serenata Endings

The night brings not just peaceful thoughts and dreams, but typically the torment of the rejected or unrequited lover. Thus two of the works in this edition include pieces portraying the fury of battle. *Perché tacete, regolati concenti?* ends with an aria in which violins play in *stile concitato* to accompany the singer's "Deh pensieri in me si schieri a battaglia." More typical an ending is the effect in the final aria of *Hor che l'aurato nume* of the voice sinking into the polyphonic string texture with a low-placed sustained note ("dammi la morte"). In this case, the final solemn movement is preceded directly by a recitative marked Presto and calling for revenge ("Su! Sdegno alla vendetta"). At the other end of the spectrum is the fade-out to silence and repose, the "addio" of *Eurilla, amata Eurilla*, and most poetic of all, the unaccompanied ascending "Addio, addio" of *Hor che di Febo ascosi*, which prophetically marks Scarlatti's farewell to the "Serenata a voce sola."

Aspects of Performance

Size of Ensemble

The most commonly cited evidence about the size of instrumental ensembles for serenata performances involves the sumptuous events in marine settings such as Posilippo, or in splendid gardens, like that described in the *Gazzetta di Napoli* for Scarlatti's 1696 composition *Il trionfo delle stagioni* with chorus, solo instruments, and ripieno instruments, reported as comprising fifty singers and one hundred and fifty instrumentalists.[19] With regard to the Roman serenata performances commissioned by Cardinal Ottoboni in the same decade, ensembles of variable size are documented by Teresa Chirico, rising from fifteen players plus a singer (1691) to garden entertainments involving over sixty instrumentalists

TABLE 1
Sleep Arias in Solo Serenatas by Alessandro Scarlatti

Serenata	Aria	Tempo; Meter	Key	Form and Instruments
Perché tacete, regolati concenti?	"Dormi, ma sappi almen" (third aria of four)	Largo; 3/4	G minor in D-MÜs (overall key of serenata, D minor); transposed to F minor in F-Pn (overall key of serenata, C minor)	Strophic, lines 1 and 2 return to complete form. Basso continuo, ritornello with two violins following each strophe.
Sotto l'ombra d'un faggio	"Io dormivo presso al rivo" (second aria of three)	no tempo marking; 3/8	B-flat major (overall key of serenata, E minor)	Da capo, with violin solo obbligato throughout aria. Ritornello introduces aria; concluding ritornello with two violins.
Notte, ch'in carro d'ombre	"Con l'idea d'un bel gioire" (third aria of four)	Adagio (Largo); 3/8	F minor (overall key of serenata, F-sharp minor)	Da capo, with long introduction. Two violins and basso continuo throughout.
Hor che di Febo ascosi	"Dormite, posate" (fourth and last aria)	Adagio; 3/4	D major (overall key of serenata, D major)	Through-composed. Two violins and basso continuo throughout.

(August 1693).[20] But such large ensembles are not connected with secular works for a solo voice, as they often involved a chorus as well as a number of solo singers. The intimate tone of the works presented in this volume suggests that the Neapolitan serenatas "a voce sola" of the 1670s, and the solo serenatas of Scarlatti that followed them, were destined for performance on a more modest scale and for a select audience, yet little information can be deduced to suggest whether there was a normal size of ensemble for such works. Regarding performances in Rome, it is worth noting that the performance for Ottoboni listed by Chirico of a serenata with solo voice and instruments (29 August 1691) had an ensemble directed by Corelli consisting of six violins, two *violette*, two *violoni*, two contrabasses, two trumpets, and harpsichord.[21] Surprisingly, no lute is mentioned for this performance, which could be explained by the presence of two trumpets—which, incidentally, rules out any of the present works by Scarlatti.

When small string ensembles are documented, for example, in paybills for Ottoboni's *accademia* of 2 May 1694, and 13 June of the same year, they probably represent ensembles for purely instrumental performance rather than for cantata accompaniment; Chirico connects these events to the recent publication of Corelli's opus 4, "Sonate a tre composte per l'Accademia dell Emin.mo e Rev.mo Signor Card. Ottoboni." But the proportions of these ensembles give a useful indication for today's performers: four violins and two violoni (2 May); six violins, two violette, and four violoni (13 June).[22] It is possible that serenatas with solo voice and two violin parts could be given with one instrument per part, but explicit documentation for this is not known to exist. Several authors—among them, Ursula Kirkendale and Reinhard Strohm—mention that patrons such as Ottoboni and Ruspoli retained some musicians as members of the household, "cameriere," who were thus not specifically engaged for performances at their *accademie*.[23] This implies that cantata performances (including solo serenatas) would not necessarily be documented in paybills of patrons such as Ottoboni and Ruspoli.

Designations of parts do not occur in these manuscripts or in the Scarlatti works presented in this volume, other than the title "Serenata a voce sola con violini" (see, e.g., *Hor che l'aurato nume*). In several of the works we find one aria with a single violin part and the heading "Violino solo," as in *Sotto l'ombra d'un faggio* (second aria, "Io dormivo presso al rivo") and *Notte, ch'in carro d'ombre* (second aria, "Veloce e labile"). The latter work also includes two *solo* markings and one *tutti* marking in the third aria ("Con l'idea d'un bel gioire"). However, these do not conclusively suggest an ensemble of more than one violin per part, as the *solo* markings coincide with vocal entries on both occasions, and with the thinning of the texture to a single violin part. More suggestive are the *solo* markings on both violin parts in the third aria of *Hor che di Febo ascosi* ("Vago fior, ch'in notte algente") in D-MÜs Hs. 3936. The virtuoso figuration and dove-tailing of the parts here certainly suggests concertino writing, contrasting with the chordal sonorities of the sinfonia (evoking Corellian style) and the simpler violin writing of the D-major arias that open and conclude the work. These works show the increasing ripieno/concertino basis of Scarlatti's scoring in the first decade of the eighteenth century. In the seventeenth-century works, the two violin parts and vocal part are often closely intertwined, the violins imitating or anticipating the phrasing and declamation of the vocal part. But in *Perché tacete, regolati concenti?* Scarlatti makes witty play on the competing claims of violins and voice, opening the work with an original and lengthy sinfonia which is virtually a trio sonata in its own right. When the singer finally enters with the ironic words "Why are you silent, concordant harmonies?," the tables are turned: the voice takes the lead while the violins accompany in short ritornelli. The work climaxes in a call to battle (the aria "Deh pensieri") which gives free rein to all the performers.

The Bass Part

Similarly, no explicit indications appear on Scarlatti's solo serenata scores to guide the choice of bass and continuo instruments. Thus decisions for performance must depend on hints from various sources on contemporary continuo practice. From the subdued and solemn tone of a number of the sinfonias and, most of all, from the "sleep arias," we may regard the archlute as essential to the sonorities of the solo serenata; this was the indispensable chord instrument of late-seventeenth-century Italian instrumental ensembles, and of course it was transportable to the various outdoor performance venues sought after for serenatas. On the other hand, the presence of a harpsichord is not excluded by the venues used for serenatas, as illustrations show,[24] in addition to the records of harpsichords being moved to particular performance venues for Cardinal Ottoboni.[25]

Throughout Scarlatti's output of vocal works with strings, but particularly from the early eighteenth century, we see the instruction "si suona senza cimbalo"[26] applied to passages of *recitativo accompagnato,* or occasionally in arias marked *pia* from the opening (rather than as an echo effect). Though none of the current works contains such a direction, the frequent appearance of such markings in other cantata and serenata scores underlines Scarlatti's preference for quiet pieces to be performed without harpsichord.

The question of the bowed bass instrument types to be preferred is of course primarily a matter of the size of ensemble, but also the period of the work and place of performance. The coexistence of the terms "violoncello," "violone," and "contrabasso" in early-eighteenth-century Roman scores is well documented.[27] Scarlatti's practice of dividing the bass part into lines notated on two separate staves is regularly found in his orchestral scores from his eighteenth-century period in Rome, often with instruments specified, for instance, "violoncello e leuto" (upper bass stave) and "violoni e contrabassi" or "contrabassi e cimbalo."[28] It is notable from the Ottoboni pay records that not only large ensembles for outdoor performances but also smaller groups during the 1690s occasionally specify violoni *and* contrabassi—in the case of the performance of 29 August 1691 cited above, two of each—providing sixteen foot pitch doubling of the bass part to an ensemble of only six violins. In Naples the term "viola" appears on personnel lists and in scores, designating not the alto viola but the violoncello; for example, the name of the Neapolitan cello/bass player Rocco Greco appears as late as 1708 with the designation "viola" in personnel lists of the Cappella Reale.[29]

Dynamic and Tempo Indications

As the early part of Scarlatti's career is the least documented in terms of autograph manuscript material, it is impossible to tell how much detail we may be missing in the extant copies from this period. Of the later works, three of the copyists represented here (those of F-Pn Rés. Vmc ms. 66 and D-MÜs 3936 and 3937) were part of the circle close to the composer in Rome in the first decade of the eighteenth century, and their scores—though not without a few errors—reflect the level of detail that one would expect to see on the composer's autographs. It is possible, too, that Scarlatti wrote more performance indications in these later works. The effect of "chiaroscuro" that he insisted was fundamental to the performance of his music is increasingly indicated through dynamic indications.[30] Also, the effect of dropping the dynamic level and the number of performers to focus attention on the vocal entry is conveyed in the markings of "Con l'idea" (third aria of *Notte, ch'in carro d'ombre*), with an alternation of *forte* and *piano* in the space of just two measures (m. 43 and m. 45), and the violin 1 part marked *solo* at the vocal entry of each section (m. 23 and m. 57).

One has only to note the abundance of performance markings on the score of the eighteenth-century work *Notte, ch'in carro d'ombre* in comparison with the low incidence of markings in the earlier serenatas in this volume to realize that a fundamental shift had taken place in the use of dynamic markings to convey poetic affects through expressive music notation. In works like *Perché tacete* and *All'hor che stanco il sole* it is the content of the score—its poetic text and musical gestures—not the presence of markings that gives clues to performance, including articulations, through the imitative writing between voice and violins.

One of the principal copyists represented by several works in this collection (*Eurilla, amata Eurilla, All'hor che stanco il sole, Prima d'esservi infedele,* and *Sotto l'ombra d'un faggio*) is considered by Mauro Amato to have been active during the 1670s and 1680s and to have been knowledgeable about both Roman and Neapolitan music.[31] His copies contain vocal slurs and a high degree of clarity in the writing and underlay of the text. Few tempo markings for arias appear, but in *Prima d'esservi infedele* a number of *piano* markings indicate echo phrase repetitions, as well as the A-flat inflected passage in "Se la sorte avesse in seno" at measures 20–24.

In the seventeenth-century serenatas of Scarlatti, it is the matching of musical idea to poetic image, rather than specific performance markings, that suggests nuances in performance. In *Perché tacete, regolati concenti?* the idea of silence recurs at strategic moments, first in the sinfonia (mm. 71–73), then within the first aria ("Alla mano che dotta in voi scherza," e.g., mm. 6, 8, and 9), and in the final recitative at the words "non puoi – nè vuoi udire – il pianto mio"—silences that portray the hesitancy of the lover whose utterances are broken before or within a lengthy outpouring of feeling. Through this example we can observe not only the ever-present interest of

Alessandro Scarlatti in portraying individual images of the poem, but his ability to create a musical idea that acts as a unifying thread throughout the structure of a whole serenata. Though these works require a high level of vocal skill, they demand of the performers even more awareness of the elements of imagery, tonal structure, and the dialogue between voice and instruments.

Notes

1. Edwin Hanley, "Alessandro Scarlatti's 'Cantate da Camera': A Bibliographical Study" (Ph.D. diss., Yale University, 1963), 369.

2. I am indebted to Dr. Mauro Amato, librarian of the Biblioteca del Conservatorio di Musica San Pietro a Majella, Naples, for drawing my attention to the late-seventeenth-century Neapolitan solo serenata repertoire, which is discussed by Dinko Fabris, "La serenata a Napoli prima di Alessandro Scarlatti," in *La serenata tra Seicento e Settecento: Musica, poesia, scenotecnica, Atti del convegno internazionale di studi, Reggio Calabria 16–17 maggio 2003*, ed. Nicolò Maccavino (Reggio Calabria: Laruffa Editore, 2007), 1:15–71.

3. A complete edition of Netti's *Nella notte più fosca* is given in Fabris, "La serenata a Napoli," 51–71 (appendix 2).

4. Mid-seventeenth-century examples of the association of C minor with night subjects include Luigi Rossi, *Hor ch'in notturna pace* (SAB and basso continuo) and Antonio Cesti's *Quanto sete per me pigri, o momenti* (S and basso continuo), ed. Rosalind Halton, Web Library of Seventeenth-Century Music (http://aaswebsv.aas.duke.edu/wlscm), no. 8, 2007.

5. Fabris, "La serenata a Napoli," 41.

6. Carolyn Gianturco notes that "Stradella is known to have used instruments to accompany an arioso directly," citing his Christmas cantata *Si apre al riso ogni labbro*. See "The When and How of Arioso in Stradella's Cantatas," in *Aspects of the Secular Cantata in Late Baroque Italy*, ed. Michael Talbot (Aldershot: Ashgate Books, 2009), 21.

7. The effect is paralleled in the recitative "Sì, sì, fuggi cor mio" of *Hor che l'aurato nume*, where a prolonged melisma on "et avvelena il core" is also set with a move to flat inflections.

8. See Rosalind Halton, "Night and Dreams: Text, Texture, and Night Themes in Cantatas by Alessandro Scarlatti," in *Music Research: New Directions for a New Century*, ed. Michael Ewans, Rosalind Halton, and John A. Phillips (London: Cambridge Scholars Press, 2004), 32–34, for a discussion of similarities between Scarlatti's cantata *Silenzio, aure volanti* and Stradella's sinfonia for *Crocifissione e Morte di N.S. Giesù Christo*.

9. Venice, Biblioteca Nazionale Marciana (I-Vnm), Cod. Marc. It. IV, 560.

10. The hand is that of Sebastien de Brossard, a notable collector of the Italian cantata repertoire. See Jean Lionnet, "Les choix italiens de Sebastien de Brossard," in *Sebastien de Brossard: Musicien*, ed. Jean Duron (Paris: Klincksieck, 1998), 13–23; on Alessandro Scarlatti, 19–20.

11. G. B. Viviani, I-Nc 33.5.35, fols. 1r–6r.

12. *Silenzio, aure volanti*, aria 3, D-MÜs 3908 and Oxford, Bodleian Library (GB-Ob), Sch. E. I. 396, ed. Rosalind Halton, http://www.cantataeditions.com.

13. See, for example, Viviani's *Di rugiadose lacrime*, I-Nc 33.4.4, fols. 141r–144r (solo voice and basso continuo), which is in the key of E-flat, with arias in F minor and A-flat.

14. Paglia's poetry was regularly set by Scarlatti in the 1690s. See Norbert Dubowy, "'Al tavolino medesimo del Compositor della Musica': Notes on Text and Context in Alessandro Scarlatti's *cantata da camera*," in *Aspects of the Secular Cantata in Late Baroque Italy*, 120–22.

15. "Ah wake, my dear eyes, do not sleep, it would be too unworthy . . ."; second strophe: "Yes, sleep, beloved eyes, do not open, it would be too beautiful . . ."

16. "You sleep, oh my love, and dream of cruelty. I wake to suffering and I think of faithfulness."; second strophe: "You sleep, and your cruel glance wounds. I wake, and my faithful breast languishes."

17. I-Nc 33.4.4, fols. 13r–20v, and Rome, Biblioteca Nazionale Centrale Vittorio Emanuele II (I-Rn), MSS Musicali 68 (RISM series A/II).

18. A fine example of a Scarlatti sleep aria occurs in the 1696 serenata *Il Genio di Partenope, la Gloria del Sebeto, il Piacere di Mergellina*, ed. Thomas Griffin (http://www.ascarlatti2010.net/main_page/genio/genio_a4.pdf); see the penultimate aria "Venticelli lenti lenti," in C minor, 3/8, which is complete with two "Echo" groups of two violins each. The text is an invocation to the breezes to be still so that Maria (viceregina of Naples) can sleep.

19. Thomas Griffin, *Musical References in the Gazzetta di Napoli, 1681–1725* (Berkeley: Fallen Leaf Press, 1993), 23–24 (Doc. 97, 31 luglio 1696).

20. Teresa Chirico, "L'inedita serenata alla Regina Maria Casimira di Polonia: Pietro Ottoboni committente di cantate e serenate (1689–1708)," in *La serenata tra Seicento e Settecento*, 2:397–449. On the size of ensembles for Ottoboni's serenata performances, see especially pp. 404–20.

21. Chirico, "L'inedita serenata," 405.

22. Chirico, "L'inedita serenata," 412–13. Sven Hostrup Hansell, "Orchestral Practice at the Court of Cardinal Pietro Ottoboni," *Journal of the American Musicological Society* 19 (1966): 398–403, remains a useful study of the proportions of string ensembles in Rome from the 1690s to the 1720s. Hans Joachim Marx, "Die Musik am Hofe Pietro Kardinal Ottobonis unter Arcangelo Corelli," *Analecta Musicologica* 5 (1968): 122–61, gives an important compilation of extracts from the Giustificazioni of the Fondo Ottoboni (Archivio Barberini).

23. The issue of musicians as members of the households of major patrons is touched upon by Hansell, "Orchestral Practice," 400; Ursula Kirkendale, "The Ruspoli Documents on Handel," *Journal of the American Musicological Society* 20 (1967): 228; Reinhard Strohm, "Handel's Italian Journey as a European Experience," in *Essays on Handel and Italian Opera* (Cambridge: Cambridge University Press, 1985), 7.

24. The designs for serenata staging in Palermo in the 1690s—clearly large ensembles for major celebrations—show harpsichords even as part of marine staging. See Anna Tedesco, "La serenata a Palermo all fine del Seicento e il Duca di Uceda," in *La serenata tra Seicento e Settecento*, 2:547–98.

25. Chirico, "L'inedita serenata," 406 n. 28.

26. For example, the opening *recitativo accompagnato* of Scarlatti's cantata *Nel silenzio commune di notte* for soprano,

xxix

two violins, viola, and basso, GB-Lbl Add. 14163, ed. Rosalind Halton, http://www.cantataeditions.com.

27. See, for example, Stefano La Via, " 'Violone' e 'Violoncello' a Roma al tempo di Corelli," *Studi Corelliani* 4 (1986): 165–91; Stephen Bonta, "Terminology for the Bass Violin in Seventeenth-Century Italy," *Journal of the American Musical Instrument Society* 4 (1978): 5–42; and Stefano La Via, "Un'aria di Händel con violoncello obbligato e la tradizione romana," in *Händel e gli Scarlatti a Roma, Atti del convegno internazionale di studi, Roma 12–14 giugno 1985*, ed. Nino Pirrotta and Agostino Ziino (Florence: Olschki, 1987), 49–71.

28. See Alessandro Scarlatti, *Venere, Adone, et Amore: Original Version, Naples 1696 and Revised Version, Rome 1706*, ed. Rosalind Halton, Recent Researches in the Music of the Baroque Era, vol. 157 (Middleton, Wis.: A-R Editions, 2009), xiii–xiv.

29. Guido Olivieri, "Cello Teaching and Playing in Naples in the Early Eighteenth Century: Francesco Paolo Supriani's *Principij da imparare a suonare il violoncello*," in *Performance Practice: Issues and Approaches*, ed. Timothy D. Watkins (Ann Arbor: Steglein Publishing, 2009), 110–11.

30. Alessandro Scarlatti to Ferdinando de' Medici, Roma, 29 maggio 1706, in I-Fas, *filza* 5903, *lettera* 204, quoted in Mario Fabbri, *Alessandro Scarlatti e il Principe Ferdinando de' Medici* (Florence: Olschki, 1961), 74.

31. Mauro Amato, "Le antologie di arie e di arie e cantate tardo-seicentesche alla Biblioteca del Conservatorio 'S. Pietro a Majella' di Napoli" (Ph.D. diss., Scuola di Paleografia e Filologia Musicale di Cremona, 1998), vol. 1, see especially pp. 42–44 and p. 95 n. 50.

Texts and Translations

Sventurati miei penzieri

[Arioso e Recitativo]

Sventurati miei penzieri,
dove ergete il volo audace?
Se credete haver mai pace,
ingannate questo core,
ch'è tropp'alto il ciel d'amore.

Fiamme, voi che m'ardete,
animate dal suon de' miei sospiri,
con lingua agoniziante
dite all'idolo mio ch'io peno amante.

Ma che sperar poss'io
da questo incendio mio?
Mio cor, sei scaltro poco
che le fiamme non danno altro che foco.

Sì, sì, pria che l'ardente
arda le pene mie,
bramo costante e fido
con arditi concenti
narrar l'alta caggion de miei tormenti.

La mia bella tiranna d'amore,
il suo nome qui pronto dirò,
s'addomanda.

O ciel, chi mi trattiene,
chi mi tronca la vita,
e chi m'ancide?
Palpitante timor
il cor m'ancide.

[Aria]

1. Se taccio, se parlo,
non spero pietà.
Son senza conforto,
se parlo, più temo,
se taccio, son morto.

2. Destino crudele,
che vuoi più da me?
Son tante le pene,
parlando e tacendo,
morir mi conviene.

My wretched thoughts,
where do you take bold flight?
If you think you will ever have peace,
you delude this heart,
since the heaven of love is too high.

You flames that burn me,
excited by the sound of my sighs,
with agonizing speech
tell my idol that I suffer as a lover.

But what can I hope
from this fire of mine?
My heart, you have little cunning
since the flames bear nothing but fire.

Yes, yes, before the burning
consumes my pain,
I, constant and faithful,
yearn to relate the noble cause of my torment
with audacious harmony.

My beautiful tyrant of love,
her name I will promptly say here,
if someone asks.

O heaven, who keeps me at bay,
who cuts short my life,
and who slays me?
Throbbing fear
kills my heart.

1. Whether I am silent or I speak,
I do not hope for mercy.
I am without comfort;
if I speak, I am all the more afraid,
if I am silent, I am dead.

2. Cruel destiny,
what more do you want from me?
The pains are so many,
both speaking and remaining silent,
to die suits me best.

Eurilla, amata Eurilla

1. [Recitativo]

Eurilla, amata Eurilla,	Eurilla, beloved Eurilla,
giunta è l'hora fatale,	the inevitable hour has arrived,
che le mete prescrive al viver mio.	which destiny dictates to my life.
Bella partir degg'io,	Oh, beautiful one, I must leave,
ma come, oh Dio,	but how, oh God,
come potrò partire	how will I be able to leave
te lasciando mio cor senza morire.	without dying, as I leave my heart with you.

2. [Aria]

Come mai partir potrò,	How will I ever be able to leave,
se non ho più core in petto,	if I no longer have a heart in my breast,
s'egli solo ha in te ricetto,	if it only has shelter in you,
come, oh Dio, non morirò?	oh God, how will I not die?
Ah lo so!	Ah, I know!
Viverò privo di core,	I will live deprived of my heart,
per rendere più acerbo	in order to render more acute
il mio dolore.	my pain.

3. Recitativo

Ma barbaro spietato	But let the cruel fate
contro me s'armi il fato.	be armed against me.
Sian pur crude e rubelle	Let the stars be cruel and rebellious
a miei danni le stelle,	to my undoing,
che d'esse non potrà l'aspro tenore	their bitter ways will not be able to untie
il nodo sciorre onde m'avvinse amore.	the knot with which love chained me.

4. [Aria]

1. Lungi ancor dal petto amante,	1. Still far from the loving breast,
questo cor t'adorerà.	this heart will adore you.
E pria d'esser incostante,	And it would meet a thousand deaths,
mille morti incontrerà.	before being unfaithful.

2. Tra le Veneri più fine,	2. Amidst the most beautiful Venuses,
arderò solo per te.	I will burn only for you.
Nè bell'occhio o vago crine	Neither alluring eyes nor ravishing hair
fiamme e lacci havrà per te.	will have the snares and the passion I have for you.

5. [Recitativo]

Eurilla, anima mia,	Eurilla, my soul, more I should say
più ti direi più giurarei ancora,	and still more I should swear to you,
ma già sorge l'Aurora,	but dawn is breaking already,
che altrui nuntia è di pace a me di pene:	which to others heralds peace, but to me it is pain:
mi costringe a lasciarti amato bene.	it forces me to leave you.
Partir conviemmi, oh Dio!	I must go, oh God!
Vado a penar,	I am going to suffer,
vado a morir,	I am going to die,
addio.	farewell.

All'hor che stanco il sole

2. [Recitativo]

All'hor che stanco il sole	At the time when the sun,
dal faticoso corso,	tired from its laborious course,
prendea dolce riposo in seno a Teti,	was taking sweet rest in the breast of Tethys,
il tradito Fileno,	the betrayed Fileno,
non trovando quiete al suo gran duolo,	not finding comfort for his great sorrow,
abbandonato e solo,	abandoned and alone,

cercò vicino al mar
con quest'accenti temprar
le fiamme al susurrar
de' venti:

3. [Aria]
"Clori bella, e dove sei?
Qual rigor d'iniquo fato,
per dar morte a un sventurato,
ti rubbò dagl'occhi miei?
Clori bella, e dove sei?"

4. [Aria]
Se del Tebro in su le sponde
godi l'hore fortunate,
io qui rendo addolorate
con il pianto ancora l'onde.

5. [Recitativo]
Misero, a che son giunto?
Imagine del duolo,
oggetto delle pene,
vivo tra lacci e stringo sol catene.
Nè spero haver conforto.
Lungi dal centro suo, Fileno è morto.

6. [Aria]
1. Deh, torna mia vita,
mia speme gradita,
che l'alma nel seno
languisce e vien meno
lontano da te.

2. Mio dolce ristoro,
mio caro tesoro,
da pace ad un core,
ch'in preda all'ardore,
ti chiede mercè.

7. [Recitativo]
Ma con chi parlo? Ahi lasso!
Con chi chiude nel petto, alma di sasso.

8. [Aria]
Aure placide e serene,
che con dolce mormorio
qui d'intorno v'aggirate,
al mio bene, al idol mio,
queste lagrime portate.

9. [Recitativo]
E dite alla crudel
che mi lasciò: "Fileno l'infelice
questo dono t'invia, così ti dice:

10. [Aria]
"Già che more un disperato,
sappi almen furia d'amore,
che l'acerbo suo dolore
lo riduce in tale stato."

tried near the sea
with these words to temper
his flames to the whispering
of the wind:

"Beautiful Clori, where are you?
What cruelty of an unjust fate,
in order to kill an unlucky man,
stole you from my eyes?
Beautiful Clori, where are you?"

If on the bank of the Tiber
you enjoy blessed hours,
here I still make the waves sorrowful
with my lament.

Wretched one, to what point have I come?
Image of sorrow,
object of pain,
I live amidst traps and I only tighten the chains.
Nor do I hope to have comfort.
Far from his goal, Fileno is dead.

1. Oh, come back my life,
my pleasing hope,
because the soul in my breast
is languishing and dying
far from you.

2. My sweet comfort,
my dear treasure,
give peace to a heart,
which, overwhelmed by passion,
asks you for mercy.

But with whom do I speak? Ah, wretch that I am!
I speak with one who holds within her breast a soul of
   stone.

Placid and serene breezes,
you that with sweet murmurs
roam here all around,
to my beloved, to my idol,
bring these tears.

And say to the cruel one
who left me: "Unhappy Fileno
sends you this gift, telling you thus:

"Since a wretch is dying,
know at least, you fury of love,
that his bitter sorrow
reduces him to such a state."

11. [Aria]

Ma se mosse a pietà d'un fido amante,
  volete che penando oggi non mora,
deh, fate ch'io rinegga il bel sembiante
  che l'alma afflitta ancor da lungi adora,
  che l'alma afflitta ancor penando adora.

But if you have pity for a faithful lover,
  and you wish that today he might not die suffering,
oh, make me reject the beautiful image
  that my afflicted soul still adores from afar,
  that my afflicted soul, still suffering, adores.

12. [Recitativo]

Bastan l'amante luci
a far ch'in un momento,
si dilegui l'ardor, fugga il tormento.

Beloved eyes are enough
to make, in a moment,
the burning vanish, the torment flee.

[Aria]

S'alla bocca del caro mio bene
più d'un bacio soave darò,
di morte lo strale, le crude catene,
temere contento non voglio più no.

If I give to the lips of my dear beloved
more than one sweet kiss,
I, happy, no longer want to fear
the arrow of death, the cruel chains.

13. [Recitativo]

O fallaci speranze
d'un moribondo cor, vani deliri,
ove pensier t'aggiri?
Partì l'ingrata, ahi, se tornar non vuole,

mora tra l'ombre un c'ha perduto il sole.

O deceptive hopes,
vain ravings of a dying heart,
where, my thought, do you wander?
The ungrateful woman left! ah, if she does not want to return,
let me, a man who has lost the sun, die midst the shades.

Hor che l'aurato nume

2. [Recitativo]

Hor che l'aurato nume
ha tuffato il suo crin nel mar spumante,
e nel suo spento lume,
giace la notte in horrido sembiante.
Io, nemico di luce,
qual ombra adolorata
immersa nell'oblio,
qui vengo a far palese
il dolor mio.

Now that the golden deity
has plunged his tresses into the foaming sea,
and has extinguished its light,
the night lies in terrible gloom.
I, the enemy of light,
like a sorrowful shadow
sunk in oblivion,
come here to give vent
to my own sorrow.

3. Aria

Se in amor col dolce incanto
m'allettasti, o mia sirena,
mi fu cara e dolce pena
l'ondeggiar in mar di pianto.

While you tempted me into love
with alluring spells, O my siren,
my sweet and welcome penalty
was to be rocked in a sea of tears.

4. Aria

Fu il tuo bel un tuono, un lampo,
che quest'alma incenerì,
con l'ardor che tutto avvampo
del mio sen nel tuo partir.

Your beauty was thunder, lightning,
that burned up this soul,
with desire that inflamed
my whole breast with your departure.

5. Aria

Ah! nascondi il tuo rigore
o tiranna mia beltà!/deità!
Se quest'alma al fin si more
sarà troppa crudeltà.

Ah! hide your severity
O my tyrant beauty!/goddess!
If this soul finally dies
it will be from too much cruelty.

6. [Aria]

Se non vuoi ch'io t'ami, o vaga,
deh! ritornami il cor mio,
che saprò con dirmi addio,
risanar l'ardente piaga.

If you don't want me to love you, O beauty,
come! Give me back my heart,
so that I will be able to heal again
the burning wound, in saying goodbye.

7. [Aria]

Alle sponde dell'onde di Lethe
già Cupido mi condannò.
Dell'ardore d'amore la sete
tutto lieto io spegnerò.

To the banks of the river Lethe
Cupid has long condemned me.
I will happily quench
the thirst of burning love.

8. Recitativo

Sì, sì, fuggi cor mio
d'una belva crudel l'horrido aspetto,
basilisco inhumano,
che con sguardi d'amore
ferisce l'alma et avvelena il core.
Su! Sdegno alla vendetta.
Provi questa tiranna!
Se mi manca di fe', se stessa inganna.

Yes, yes, flee, my heart,
from the terrible vision of a cruel beast,
inhuman basilisk,
that with looks of love
wounds the soul and poisons the heart.
Arise! May revenge become disdain.
Challenge this tyrant!
If she does not believe me, she betrays herself.

Così risoluto amore,
così conchiudo, oh Dio,
benché piaga mortal resti al cor mio.

Such a resolute love,
thus I decide, oh God,
though a fatal wound remains in my heart.

9. [Aria]

Ah! fiera sorte,
se pace mi vuoi dar, dammi la morte.

Ah! Harsh fate,
if you want to give me peace, give me death.

Prima d'esservi infedele

1. [Introdutione]

Prima d'esservi infedele,
luci belle, io morirò.
Face ardente e stral crudele
sol per voi soffrir saprò.

Before being unfaithful to you,
beautiful eyes, I will die.
The burning torch and the cruel dart
I shall endure only for you.

Duri laci, aspri affanni,
sono atroci tiranni a un alma amante.

Harsh chains, bitter troubles,
are terrible tyrants to a loving soul.

2. Recitativo

Ma se con bella fede,
nel penar, nel soffrir, vive costante,
perde l'orrido aspetto ogn'empia pena
e divien libertà la sua catena.

But if with proper faith,
in the torment, in the suffering,
each cruel pain lives faithfully,
it loses its terrible aspect and its chain becomes freedom.

Io, che ancor fui piagata
dal crudo stral del pargoletto arciero,
piango, sospiro, è vero,
ma perché fido è il core,
di soave piacere
prende grata sembianza il mio dolore.

I, who was wounded again
by the cruel dart of the childish archer,
weep, sigh, it is true,
but because the heart is faithful,
my sorrow pleasingly
takes on a semblance of sweet pleasure.

Onde, per quante gioie
sa dispensar con altri dardi Amore,
io cangiar non saprai
una lagrima sol degl'occhi miei.

Therefore, in spite of the many joys
Cupid can share by means of other darts,
I shall not shed
a single tear from my eyes.

3. Aria

1. Quando sorge l'aurora
dal Gange tosto piange,
ma le stille che spargon gl'albori,
benché figlie d'acerbi cordogli,
sovra il prato nutriscono i fiori,
et ingemmano nel mare gli scogli.

1. When the dawn rises
from the East it cries immediately,
but the drops that are shed on the trees,
even if they are born of bitter grief,
nourish the flowers upon the meadow,
and adorn the rocks in the sea.

2. Spesso l'alma in dolce tormento
pianger sento,
e cadendo dal ciglio che geme
mesto pianto, tributo d'amore,
mi nutrisce nel petto la speme,
e m'ingemmano lo scoglio del core.

4. [Recitativo]
Lieta, lieta così
dell'amor mio rimango,
ed è mio preggio, e non viltà, s'io piango.
Ah, che non è possibile, no,
ch'io giammai ti tradisca, idolo amato,
con ardimento orribile!

S'io ti sono infedel, m'oltraggi il fato:
da qual altra saetta e da qual nodo
esser può l'alma mia ferita e presa?
Come altra fiamma accesa
a questo cor, si renderà insoffribile!
Ah, che non è possibile!

5. Aria
Se la sorte avesse in seno
vaghe gemme e rio veleno,
e l'offrisse, a gl'occhi miei,
poi dicesse: "Ascolta o Clori,
s'al tuo ben non sei costante
io ti dono i miei tesori;
ma se tu sei fida amante,
il velen lambisci e mori."
Tutta lieta all'hor direi:
"Ricca è vero la mercede,
ma t'inganni, o cieca sorte:
Pria ch'offender la mia fede,
voglio sugger la mia morte."

6. Recitativo
Esempio di costanza
sarò nel mondo, e s'armi temerario
destino contro me
con tirannia crudele,
ch'ognor costante all'idol mio dirò:

"Prima d'esservi infedele,
luci belle, io morirò."

Perché tacete, regolati concenti?

2. [Recitativo]
Perché tacete,
regolati concenti?
Seguite pur a lusingare il cor
ne' suoi tormenti.

3. Aria
1. Alla mano che dotta in voi scherza,
quanto è simile il Nume d'Amor,
e con l'arco d'un ciglio mi sferza,
et unisce la gioia al dolor.

2. Often in sweet torment
I feel my soul crying,
and falling from my lamenting eye
a sad tear, a tribute of love,
nourishes the hope in my breast,
and adorns the rock of my heart.

Therefore I remain happy
about my love,
and it is to my credit, and not cowardice, if I weep.
Ah, how impossible it is
that I could ever betray you,
with terrible boldness, beloved idol!

If I am unfaithful to you, may fate revile me:
from what other dart and from what knot
could my soul be wounded and captured?
How could another flame be kindled
to this heart, it would be insufferable!
Ah, how impossible it is!

If fate were to have in its breast
beautiful gems and wicked poison,
and were to offer them before my eyes,
then saying: "Listen, O Clori,
if you are not constant to your beloved
I will give you my treasures;
but if you are a faithful lover,
you will lap up the poison and die."
Completely happy then I would say:
"Plentiful, it is true, is your offer,
but you delude yourself, O blind fate:
Before ever offending my faith,
I want to sip my death."

I shall be an example of constancy
in the world, and let fool-hardy destiny
take up arms against me
with cruel tyranny,
because always constant to my idol, I will say:

"Before being unfaithful to you,
beautiful eyes, I will die."

Why are you silent,
concordant harmonies?
Continue to entice my heart
in its torments.

1. How similar is the God of Love
to the hand that teases you skillfully,
and strikes me with the bow of his arched brow,
and unites joy with pain.

2. Con l'argento di guancia fiorita,
tesse i stami a quest'alma il desir,
e all'invito di speme gradita,
corrisponde armonia di sospir.

4. [Recitativo]
Ma che dissi? Tacete!
In immagin più bella,
vada vivo il tenore
di mia sorte rubella.

Sì, sì, che del mio ben ne vaghi lumi
ha il mio ardore il suo loco.
Nè sia stupor che brilli
entro i raggi d'un sole il mio bel foco.

5. [Aria]
1. Tra le fiamme del mio duolo,
scenda a volo
un sol raggio di tua beltà.
E sarà la bell'iride al mio core,
quell'ardore
ch'aspra guerra nel petto mi fa.

2. Dall'ardor dei tuoi bei lumi,
si consumi,
freddo gel che mi serpe nel sen.
E 'l balen d'un tuo sguardo lusinghiero
sia foriero
a quest'alma d'un giorno seren.

6. [Recitativo]
Nè m'ascolti, crudele,
così le tue vittorie
o non curi o disprezzi.
Scopri del tuo poter le forze homai
fia ch'ogni orror disgombre.
Farai nascer il giorno,
in mezzo all'ombre.

Ah, che ben io v'intendo,
stelle d'amor nemiche.
Per tormentare i miei pensieri amanti
volete anco sprezzare i propri vanti.

7. [Aria]
1. Dormi, ma sappi almen
che per te moro.
E al dolce tuo sopor
entro di questo sen,
veglia il martoro.
Dormi, ma sappi almen
che per te moro.

2. Dormi, ch'il mio dolor
nenia al tuo sonno.
Forse ne' sogni ancor,
cruda, ti saprò dir:
"Te sola adoro."
Dormi, ma sappi almen
che per te moro.

2. With the sheen of a blushing cheek,
desire entwines this soul,
and to the invitation of pleasing hope,
answers the harmony of sighs.

But what have I said? Silence!
In a more beautiful image,
may the form of my rebellious fate
carry on its life.

Yes, yes, my passion has its place
in my beloved's beautiful eyes.
Nor should it astonish that my fine flame
shines midst the rays of the sun.

1. Midst the flames of my sorrow,
let descend in flight
a lone ray of your beauty.
And that which wages cruel war in my breast,
that burning
will become a rainbow to my heart.

2. Let the burning of your beautiful eyes
consume the freezing ice
that encircles my heart.
And let the lightning of your flattering gaze
be the herald
of a serene day to this soul.

But you don't hear me, cruel one,
thus you neither heed nor scorn
your victories.
Now display the force of your power
and let all horrors clear away.
You will make the day be born,
in the middle of the shadows.

Ah, how well I understand you,
hostile stars of love.
To torment my loving thoughts
you even want to vilify your own glories.

1. Sleep, but at least know
that I am dying for you.
And over your sweet slumber
from within this heart,
torment keeps watch.
Sleep, but at least know
that I am dying for you.

2. Sleep, since my pain
is a lullaby to your sleep.
Perhaps even in dreams,
cruel one, I will know how to say to you:
"Only you I adore."
Sleep, but at least know
that I am dying for you.

8. [Recitativo]

Ma tiranna, tu dormi	But tyrant, you sleep
e tra le sopori o Dio,	and midst slumber, O God,
non puoi nè vuoi udire il pianto mio.	you neither can nor want to hear my lament.

9. [Aria]

1. Deh pensieri / in me si schieri / a battaglia, / il fiero stuol. / Et assaglia / il duro core / che l'ardore / del mio amor / sentir non vuol. / Deh pensieri / in me si schieri / a battaglia, / il fiero stuol.

1. Oh let the proud troop / of my thoughts / be drawn up / in battle-array. / And assail / the hard heart / that does not want to feel / the passion / of my love. / Oh let the proud troop / of my thoughts / be drawn up / in battle-array.

2. Se riposo / io più non oso / a domandare, / il Dio d'Amor, / col destare, / chi m'inpiaga / la mia piaga / proverà / men crudo il duol. / Deh pensieri / in me si schieri / a battaglia, / il fiero stuol.

2. Since I no longer / dare to ask / for respite, / the God of Love / will make / my wound / less painful / by awakening the one / who is inflicting it. / Oh let the proud troop / of my thoughts / be drawn up / in battle-array.

Sotto l'ombra d'un faggio

1. [Introdutione]

Sotto l'ombra d'un faggio,	Under the shade of a beech tree,
sul margine d'un rivo	on the bank of a river
in braccio al sonno, stava Fileno,	in the arms of sleep, was Fileno,
abbandonato e solo.	abandoned and alone.
Quando scosso dal duolo,	As he was hiding from sorrow,
par che havea sognato	it seems that he had dreamed
d'esser incatenato.	of being enchained.
Balzò da terra, e come alcun l'udisse,	He leapt from the ground, and as if someone could hear him,
ad occhi chiusi alzò le voci e disse:	with eyes closed he raised his voice and said:

2. Aria

Scioglietemi,	Release me,
lasciatemi,	let me go,
ch'è troppo crudeltà.	this is too much cruelty.
Rendetemi,	Grant me,
donatemi	give me
la cara libertà.	sweet liberty.

3. Recitativo

Pietà, pietà lasciate!	Oh pity, let me be!
Ei replicar volea,	He wanted to reply,
ma gl'occhi aprendo,	but opening his eyes,

e scorto ch'al ruscello	and perceiving that at the brook
alle piante egli parlava,	he was speaking to the plants,
s'avvide che sognava.	he realized that he was dreaming.
E allor ch'impatiente,	And then so impatiently,
col ciglio dispettoso,	with a scornful look,
già consigliava il fianco.	already he was turning to his side.
A novello riposo,	In his new repose,
vide Filli la vaga e non fu sogno.	he saw the beautiful Filli and it was not a dream.
Onde, ver lei movendo	Therefore, moving towards her
ben frettoloso il passo,	with a very hasty step,
persuadeva così quel cor di sasso:	he was persuading that heart of stone like this:

4. Aria

Io dormivo	I was sleeping
presso al rivo	by the river
e sognai,	and I dreamed,
ma non errai,	but I did not err,
che m'haveano incatenato	that they had enchained me
mentre son vicino a te!	whilst I was close to you!
Ha ragione	My enraptured
il mio core	heart
innamorato,	is right,
ch'è prigione della fe'.	since it is the prisoner of faithfulness.

5. Recitativo

Ragione ha il cor,	My heart is right,
ma il labro non ha ragion.	but my lips are not.
Se esclama,	If they exclaim—
per haver libertade,	in order to have freedom,
e star disciolto	and be released
su l'altar del tuo volto,	before the altar of your face—
i delirii del labro,	these ravings of my lips,
o bella, io sveno;	O beautiful one, I faint;
e se giammai ricusera d'amarti,	and if ever they will deny loving you,
per reo dichiaro il seno.	I will declare my heart guilty.

6. Aria

Talvolta il dolore,	Sometimes sorrow,
che d'esser felice	which does not believe in the hope
non crede alla speme,	of being happy,
si sente sul labro	hears itself on the lips
chiamar libertà.	calling for freedom.
Che fugga le pene	So that it may flee the pains
del regno d'amore,	of the kingdom of love,
il labro lo dice,	the lips say so,
ma il cor non lo sa.	but the heart does not know it.

Notte, ch'in carro d'ombre

2. [Recitativo]

Notte, ch'in carro d'ombre	Night, you who in shadowy chariot
per l'aerei sentier raggiri il corso,	wend your way through airy paths,
veloce oltre l'usato	quicker than usual
con la sferza di stelle	with the lash of the stars
a' tuoi bruni destrier flagelli il dorso.	you whip the backs of your black horses.
E rallentato il morso	And, having slackened the bit
mentre rapida scorri	while you fly rapidly
entro l'etere[a] mole, guidami, o cara Notte,	through ethereal space, lead me, O dear Night,
in grembo al sole.	into the bosom of the sun.

3. [Aria]

Vieni, o Notte, e in questo petto
faccian tregua i rei martiri.
E sian guida al caro oggetto
l'aure sol de' miei sospiri.

4. [Recitativo]

E tu, ch'ognor ti vanti
fuggir senza ritorno
e de' proprii tuoi parti esser tiranno,
ingratissimo Tempo,
perché non togli un anno
di pene a me per far più breve un giorno?
Perché non copri i rai
col tuo bel manto al dì, Notte, che fai?
Vuol forse il Dio dell'ore
per dar piena vittoria al mio dolore,
fermar il Plaustro, e rinovar portenti.
Deh, non tardate più, pigri momenti.

5. [Aria]

Veloce e labile
fugge e dileguasi
il giorno e 'l sol.
Per esser fiere
contro il mio core,
si ferman l'ore,
posan le sfere
sol per mio duol.

6. Recitativo

Ma parmi ch'esaudite
renda le mie preghiere,
e con oscuro vel Notte pietosa
invita ogni mortale a prender posa.
Dormi, dormi, Amarilli,
sol vegli questo core
ove scolpì di Tirsi
la bella imago Amore.
E sogni l'alma amante
quei piacer, quei diletti,
che godere non può fuor del riposo.
Quindi tacciano intanto
i miei sospiri e 'l mormorio del pianto.

7. [Aria]

Con l'idea d'un bel gioire,
dolce sonno, vieni a me.
E con l'ombra sì gradita
del mio sol, della mia vita,
dona tregua al mio martire,
lusingando la mia fe'.

8. [Recitativo]

Ma voi non vi chiudete,
mie dolenti pupille? Ohimè, che fia?
Ah' ben l'intendo, sì: l'anima mia
solo avvezza ai martiri,
non conosce riposo.

Come, O Night, and to this breast
may cruel torments give respite.
And to my beloved object let
the breezes of my sighs be the sole guide.

And you, who always boast
of fleeing without return
and of being a tyrant to your own offspring,
most ingrate Time,
why do you not rid me of a year
of pain by making a day shorter?
Why don't you cover the rays of day
with your beautiful mantle, Night, what are you doing?
Perhaps the God of hours,
to give full victory to my suffering,
will halt the Big Dipper, and renew its portents.
Oh, delay no longer, sluggish moments.

Swiftly and smoothly
flees and fades
the light of day.
To be cruel
to my heart,
the hours stand still,
the spheres halt
only for my grief.

But it seems to me that
my prayers are granted,
and with dark veil merciful Night
invites every mortal to take rest.
Sleep, sleep, Amarilli,
may only this heart remain awake
on which Cupid has etched
the beautiful image of Tirsi.
And may the noble lover dream
of those pleasures, those delights,
that she cannot enjoy except when asleep.
Therefore let my sighs be silent,
and the murmuring of my weeping.

With the idea of great pleasure,
sweet sleep, come to me.
And with the shadow so beloved
of my sun, of my life,
give pause to my suffering,
beguiling my faith.

But are you not closed,
my suffering eyes? Alas, what may be?
Ah, well I understand, yes: my soul,
only accustomed to my torments,
does not know rest.

Sì, sì, veglia Amarilli,	Yes, yes, Amarilli is awake,
e i tuoi sospiri	and if your sighs
se tregua aver non ponno,	cannot have pause,
avrà riposo il tuo dolore interno	your inner pain will have rest
quando le luci chiuderai in eterno.	when your eyes close in eternity.

9. [Aria]

Sì che priva di contento,	Thus deprived of contentment,
goderò del mio morir.	I shall enjoy my dying.
Se goder non posso in vita	If I cannot enjoy in life
la cagion del mio tormento,	the cause of my torment,
sol la morte mi è gradita	only death is welcome to me
come fine al mio martir.	as the end of my pining.

Text edited and translated by Barbara Sachs.

Hor che di Febo ascosi

2. Recitativo

Hor che di Febo ascosi	Now that the splendid rays of Phoebus
stanno in sen d'Anfitrite i rai splendenti,	are hidden in the breast of Amphitrite,
non fia stupor se negl'altrui riposi	be not astonished if in the repose of others
con sonori concenti	I temper my sorrows
vo temprando il mio duolo,	with harmonious sounds,
ch'è proprio degl'amanti	for it is customary for lovers,
fra solitarii orrori	in dreadful solitude,
spiegar del core i più secreti amori.	to reveal the most secret loves of their hearts.

3. Aria

Cara notte, che i furti giocondi	Dear night, you who give kindly cover
degl'amanti benigna ricopri.	to the jesting thefts of lovers.
Ben puoi tu quei diletti ch'ascondi	You may well number those hidden delights
numerar con le stelle che scopri.	along with the stars that you reveal.

4. Recitativo

Ma chi m'addita, o Dio,	But who shows me, O God,
del bell'idolo mio	among these shadows of night
fra quest'ombre notturne il viso adorno?	the fair face of my sweet beloved?
Voi sol potete il giorno	You alone can bring back the day
recar se vi destate, occhi ridenti,	if you awaken, laughing eyes,
s'havete eguale al sole i raggi ardenti.	for you burn with equal radiance to the sun.

5. Aria

Sì, sì, non dormite,	Yes, yes, sleep not,
pupille amorose.	lovely eyes.
Ch'il vostro splendore	For your brightness
dà vita a quest'alma	gives life to my soul
e brugia il mio core	and burns my heart
con faci gradite,	with welcome torches,
con fiamme di rose.	with rosy flames.

6. Recitativo

Quindi dai vostri sguardi il mio martoro	So your glances bring to my suffering
gode in mezzo ai sospir dolce ristoro.	sweet relief in the midst of my sighs.

7. Aria

Vago fior, ch'in notte algente	A lovely flower, which in the chilly night
languir freddo in terra suole,	oft languishes cold in the ground,
sol risorge all'or che sente	only arises when it feels
riscaldarsi ai rai del sole.	warmed again by the sun's rays.

8. Recitativo

Ma no, riposa o bella,	But no, sleep, O lovely one,
ch'anche dormendo ascolterai mie pene,	for even as you sleep you will hear my pains,
e fra notturne scene	and in the theater of the night
con accesa favella,	with words of fire,
saprà mostrarti il mio trafitto core,	the God of Love, in phantasmic form,
divenuto fantasma il Dio d'Amore.	will be able to show you my pierced heart.

9. Aria

Dormite, posate,	Sleep, rest,
pupille adorate,	beloved eyes,
in placido oblio.	in peaceful oblivion.
Dorma il vostro splendor ch'io parto. Addio.	Let your radiance sleep for I am leaving. Farewell!

Text edited and translated by Nerida Newbigin.

Plate 1. Alessandro Scarlatti, *Sventurati miei penzieri* (H. 710), opening measures (I-PAc, Sanv. B.1/CF-VI-44). Reproduced by kind permission of Conservatorio di Musica A. Boito, Parma.

Plate 2. Alessandro Scarlatti, *Prima d'esservi infedele* (H. 578), title page (I-MC, 5-F-4b). Scribe B, Naples. Reproduced by kind permission of Archivio dell'Abbazia di Montecassino.

Plate 3. Alessandro Scarlatti, *Prima d'esservi infedele* (H. 578), ending to introduction with arioso "Duri lacci" (I-Fc, f-I.33, previously D.2364). Reproduced by kind permission of Conservatorio Statale di Musica Luigi Cherubini, Florence.

Plate 4. Alessandro Scarlatti, *Perché tacete, regolati concenti?* (H. 551), from aria "Tra le fiamme del mio duolo," strophe 2 (D-MÜs, Hs. 3910). Copyist XIII, Rome. Reproduced by kind permission of Santini-Bibliothek, Münster.

Plate 5. Alessandro Scarlatti, *Sotto l'ombra d'un faggio* (H. 678), start of recitative "Ragione ha il cor" (I-MC, 5-F-4c). Scribe B, Naples. Reproduced by kind permission of Archivio dell'Abbazia di Montecassino.

Plate 6. Alessandro Scarlatti, *Sotto l'ombra d'un faggio* (H. 678), from aria "Talvolta il dolore," end of work (I-MC, 5-F-4c). Scribe B, Naples. Reproduced by kind permission of Archivio dell'Abbazia di Montecassino.

Plate 7. Alessandro Scarlatti, *Notte, ch'in carro d'ombre* (H. 480), from aria "Vieni, o Notte" (D-MÜs, Hs. 3937). Reproduced by kind permission of Santini-Bibliothek, Münster.

Plate 8. Alessandro Scarlatti, *Notte, ch'in carro d'ombre* (H. 480), end of recitative "Ma parmi ch'esaudite" and start of aria "Con l'idea d'un bel gioire" (D-MÜs, Hs. 3937). Reproduced by kind permission of Santini-Bibliothek, Münster.

Plate 9. Alessandro Scarlatti, *Hor che di Febo ascosi* (H. 511), from aria "Cara notte" (D-MÜs, Hs. 3936). Reproduced by kind permission of Santini-Bibliothek, Münster.

Plate 10. Alessandro Scarlatti, *Hor che di Febo ascosi* (H. 511), from aria "Vago fior, ch'in notte algente" (D-MÜs, Hs. 3936). Reproduced by kind permission of Santini-Bibliothek, Münster.

Serenate a voce sola

Sventurati miei penzieri
Serenata a voce sola di canto

[Arioso e Recitativo] — [Aria]

Edited by Marie-Louise Catsalis

19
pa- ce, in- gan- na- te que- sto co- re, in- gan- na- te que- sto
23
co- re, ch'è trop- p'al- to, ch'è trop- p'al- to il ciel d'a- mo- re,
27
ch'è trop- p'al- to, ch'è trop- p'al- to il ciel d'a- mo- re, è il
31
ciel
34
d'a- mo- re. Fiam- me, voi che m'ar- de- te, a- ni- ma- te dal suon de' miei so-
38
-spi- ri, con lin- gua a- go- ni- zian- te di- te al- l'i- do- lo mi- o, di- te al- l'i- do- lo mi- o ch'io pe-

-no, ch'io pe- - no, ch'io pe- no a- man- te. Ma che

sperar poss'i- o da questo incen- di- o mi- o? Mio cor, sei scal- tro

po- co che le fiam- me non dan- no al- tro che fo- co. Sì,

sì, pria che l'ar- den- te ar- da le pe- ne mi- e, bra- mo co- stan- te e fi- do con ar-

a tempo

-di- ti con- cen- ti nar- rar l'al- ta cag- gion de miei tor- men-

- ti, de miei tor- men- ti, nar- rar l'al- ta cag-

-gion de miei tormenti, de miei tormenti.

La mia bella tiranna d'amore, la mia bella tiranna d'amore, il suo nome qui pronto dirò, il suo nome, il suo nome, il suo nome qui pronto dirò, s'addomanda. O ciel, chi mi trattiene, chi mi tronca la vita, e chi m'ancide? Palpi-

-tan- te ti- mor il cor, il cor, il cor m'an-ci- de.

V.S. Volti per l'aria

Grave

1. Se tac- cio, se par- lo, non spe- ro pie- tà. Se tac- cio, se par- lo, non spe- ro pie- tà, no, no, non spe- ro pie- tà. Son sen- za con- for- to, se par- lo, più te- mo, se tac- cio, son mor- to, son mor- to. Son sen- za con- for- to, se par- lo, più

te- mo, se tac- cio, son mor- to, son mor- to, se tac- cio, son mor- to, son mor- to.

Grave
2. De- sti- no cru- de- le, che vuoi più da me? De- sti- no cru- de- le, che vuoi più da me? che, che, che vuoi più da me? Son tan- te le pe- ne, par- lan- do e ta- cen- do, mo- rir mi con-

IL FINE

Eurilla, amata Eurilla
Serenata a voce sola

1. [Recitativo]

Eu- ril- la, a- ma- ta Eu- ril- la, giunt'a è l'hora fa- ta- le, che le me- te pre- scri- ve al____ vi- ver mi- o.___ Bel- la par- tir deg- g'i- o, ma co- me, oh Di- o, co- me po- trò par- ti- re te la- scian- do mio cor, te la- scian- do mio cor sen- za mo- ri- re, te la- scian- do mio cor, te la- scian- do mio cor sen- za mo- ri- re.

Segue

Edited by Marie-Louise Catsalis

2. [Aria]

Co- me mai par- tir po- trò, se non ho più co- re in pet- to, non ho più cor, se non ho più cor in pet- to, s'e- gli so- lo ha in te ri- cet- to, co- me, oh Di- o, non mo- ri- rò? non mo- ri- rò? co- me, oh Dio, non mo- ri- rò? Ah lo so! Ah lo so! Vi- ve- rò pri- vo di co- re, per ren- de- re più a- cer- bo il mio do- lo- re, il mio do- lo- re.

Vi-ve-rò pri-vo di co-re, per ren-de-re più a-cer-bo il mio do-lo-re, il mio do-lo-re.

3. Recitativo

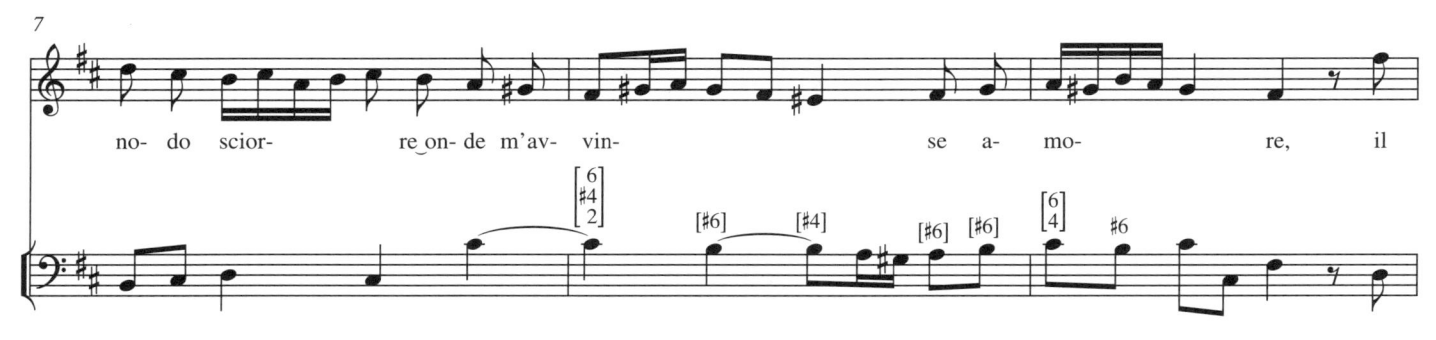

Ma bar-ba-ro spie-ta-to con-tro me s'ar-mi il fa-to. Sian pur cru-de e ru-bel-le a miei dan-ni le stel-le, che d'es-se non po-trà l'as-pro te-no-re il no-do scior-re on-de m'av-vin-se a-mo-re, il

*See critical note.

12

nodo scior- re onde m'av- vin- se a- mo- re.

4. [Aria]

1. Lun- gi an- cor dal petri- to a- man- te, questo cor,
2. Tra le Vene- ri più fi- ne, ar- de- rò,

questo cor t'a- dolo- re- rà, t'a- dolo- re- rà, t'a- per-
ar- de- rò so- lo per te, per te, per te, per

-do- re- rà, questo cor t'a- dolo- re- rà. E pria
te, per te, ar- de- rò so- lo per te. Nè bel-

d'es- ser in- co- stan- te, mil- le mor- ti, mil- le
-l'oc- chio o vago cri- ne mil fiam- me e lac- ci, mil fiam- me e

[Repeat for strophe 2]

5. [Recitativo]

Eurilla, anima mia, più ti direi più giurarei ancorra, ma già sorge l'Aurora, che altrui nuntia è di pace a me di pene: mi costringe a lasciarti amato bene. Partir convienmi, oh Dio! *Largo* Vado a penar, vado a morir, vado a penar, vado a morir, addio.

FINE

All'hor che stanco il sole
Serenata a voce sola [con violini]

1. [Sinfonia]

Edited by Marie-Louise Catsalis

2. [Recitativo]

Al- l'hor che stan- co il so- le dal fa- ti- co- so

corso, pren- de- a dol- ce ri- po- so in se- no a Te- ti, il tra-
-di- to Fi- le- no, non tro- van- do qui- e- te al suo gran
duo- lo, ab- ban- do- na- to e so- lo, cer- cò vi- ci- no al mar
con que- st'ac- cen- ti tem- prar le fiam- me al su- sur-
-rar de' ven- ti, tem- prar le
fiam- me al su- sur- rar

— de'ven- ti:

3. [Aria]

"Clo- ri bel- la, Clo- ri bel- la, e do- ve se- i?

4
e — do- ve se- i? Clo- ri bel- la, bel- la, e do- ve — se- i? —
6 [7]
8
e — do- ve se- i? —
[7]
12
Qual ri- gor — d'i- ni- quo fa- to, — per dar mor- te a un sven- tu-
[♮]
15
-ra- to, ti rub- bò — da- gl'oc- chi mie- i? Clo- ri
[♮] (♮) [♮]

20

4. [Aria]

Se del Tebro in su le spon- de
go- di l'ho- re for- tu- na- te,
go- di l'ho- re for- tu- na- te,
io qui ren- do ad- do- lo- ra- te
con il pian- to, con il pian- to
an- co- ra l'on- de, io qui

ren- do ad- do- lo- ra- te con il

pian- to, con il pian- to an- co- ra

[♭6] [6] [♯]

l'on- [de.]

[♯]

5. [Recitativo]

Mi- se-ro, a che son giun- to? I- ma- gi-ne del duo- lo, og--get- to del- le pe- ne, vi- vo tra lac- ci e strin- go sol

6. [Aria]

ca- te- -ne. Nè spe- ro ha- ver con- for- to, nè spe- ro ha- ver con- for- to. Lun- gi dal cen- tro su- o, Fi- le- no è mor- to.

1. Deh, tor- na mia vi- ta, deh, tor- na mia vi- ta, mia spe- me gra- di- ta, che l'al- ma nel se- no lan-
2. Mio dol- ce ri- sto- ro, mio dol- ce ri- sto- ro, mio ca- ro te- so- ro, da pa- ce ad un co- re, ch'in

13
-gui- sce‿e vien me- no lon- ta- no da te,
pre- da‿al- l'ar- do- re, ti chie- de mer- cè,
19
lon- ta- no da te,
ti chie- de mer- cè,
25
lan- gui- sce‿e vien me- no lon- ta- no da te,
ch'in pre- da‿al- l'ar- do- re, ti chie- de mer- cè,
31
lon- ta- -
ti chie- -

-no, lon- ta- no da te.
-de, ti chie- de mer- cè.

[Repeat from m. 1 for strophe 2]

7. [Recitativo]

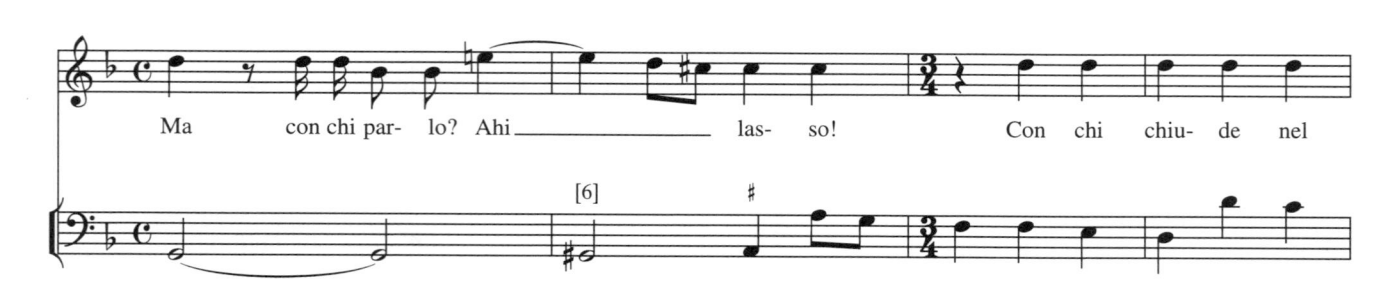

Ma con chi par- lo? Ahi las- so! Con chi chiu- de nel pet- to, al- ma di sas- so.

8. [Aria]

[Ritornello]

27

Au- re ____ pla- ci- de e se- re- ne, ___

au- re ____ pla- ci- de e se- re- ne, ___ che con ___ dol- ce ___ mor- mo- ri- o ___

qui d'in- tor- no ___ v'ag- gi- ra- - te,

al mio bene, al idol mio, queste lagrime porta-te, al mio bene, al idol mio, queste lagrime porta-te.

Ritornello ut supra

9. [Recitativo]

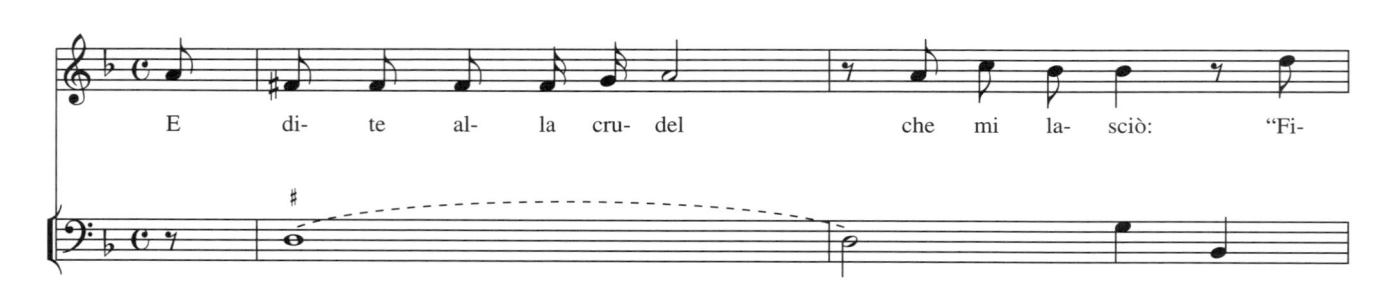

E dite alla crudel che mi lasciò: "Fi-leno l'infelice questo dono t'invia, così ti dice:

10. [Aria]

"Già che mo- re, già che mo- re un di- spe- ra- to, già che mo- re un di- spe- -ra- to, sap- pi_al- men fu- ria d'a- mo- re, che l'a- cer- bo suo do- lo- re, che l'a-

-cer- bo suo do- lo- re lo ri- du- ce in ta- le sta- to,

sap-pi_al- men fu- ria d'a-

-mo- re, sap-pi_al- men fu- ria d'a- mo- re, che l'a- cer- bo suo do-

-lo- re, che l'a- cer- bo suo do- lo- re lo ri- du- ce in ta- le

11. [Aria]

sta- to."

Ma se mosse a pietà d'un fido amante, vo- le- te che penan- do oggi non mo- ra, deh, fa- te ch'io ri--neg- ga il bel sem- bian- te che l'al- ma af- flit- ta an--cor da lun- gi_a- do- ra, che l'al- ma af--flit- ta an- cor pe- nan- do_a- do- ra.

12. [Recitativo] — [Aria]

Ba- stan l'a- man- te lu- ci a far ch'in un mo- men- to, si di- le- gui l'ar- dor, si di- le- gui l'ar- dor, fug- ga il tor- men- to.

S'al- la boc- ca del ca- ro mio be- ne___ più d'un ba- cio so- a- ve da- rò, più d'un ba- cio, più d'un bacio so- a- ve da- rò, di mor- te lo stra- le, le cru- de ca- te- ne, te- me- re con- ten- to non vo- glio più no, no,___ no, no,___ no, te- me- re con- ten- to non vo- glio più no. S'al- la boc- ca del ca- ro mio be- ne___ più d'un bacio so- a- ve da- rò, più d'un ba- cio,___ più d'un ba- cio,___ più d'un ba- cio so- a- ve da- rò.

Ritornello ut supra

13. [Recitativo]

O fal- la- ci spe- ran- ze d'un mo- ri- bon- do cor, va- ni de- li- ri, o- ve pen- sier t'ag- gi- ri? Par- tì l'in- gra- ta, ahi, se tor- nar non vuo- le, mo- ra tra l'om- bre, mo- ra tra l'om- bre un c'ha per- du- to il

sole,

mo- ra tra l'om- bre, mo- ra tra l'om- bre un c'ha per- du- to,

un c'ha per- du- to il so- le, un c'ha per- du- to il so- le.

FINE

Hor che l'aurato nume
Serenata a voce sola con violini

1. Sonata

Edited by Marie-Louise Catsalis

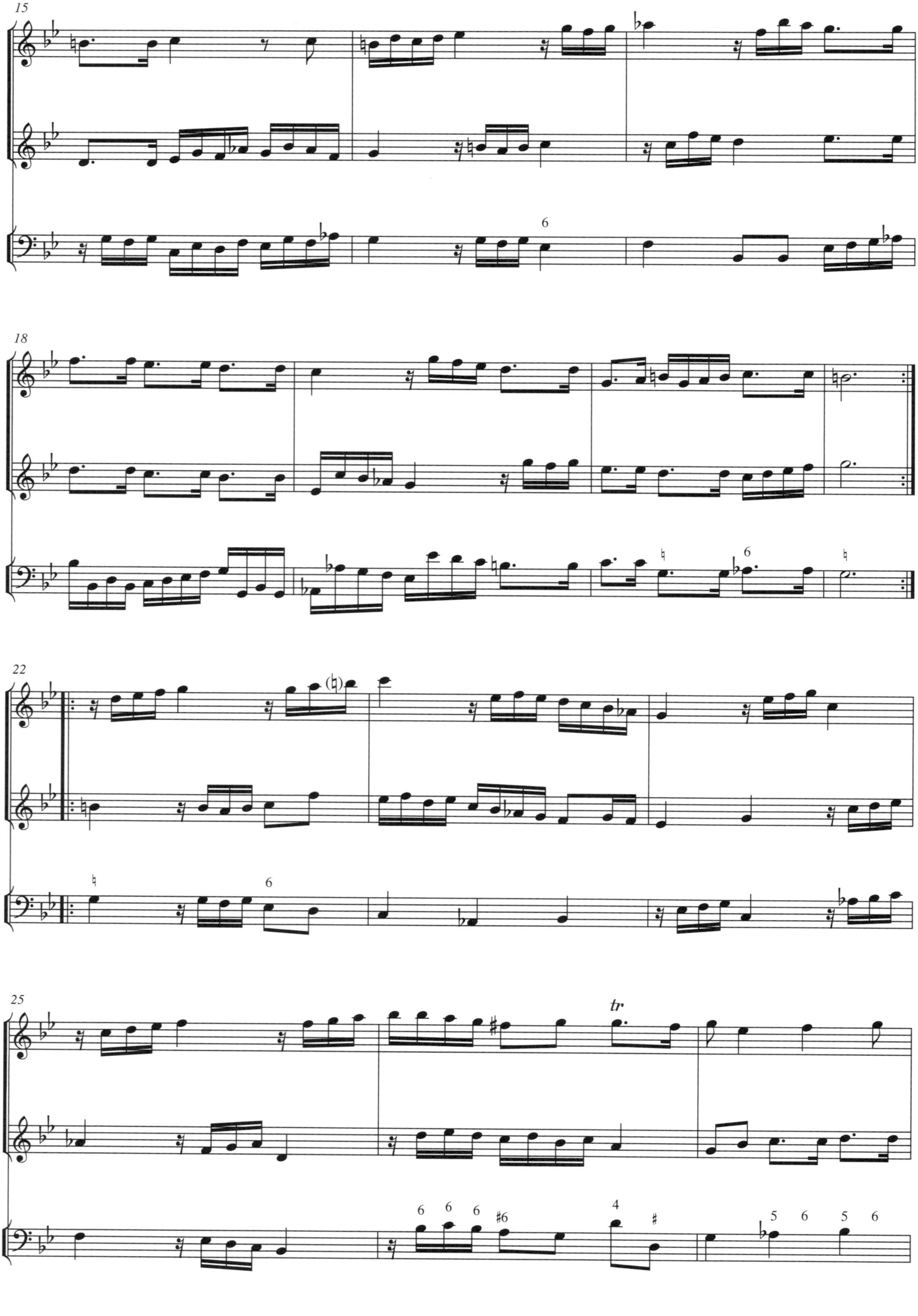
15
18
22
25
tr

2. [Recitativo]

Hor che l'au- ra- to nu- me ha tuf- fa- to il suo crin nel mar spu- man- te, e nel suo spen- to lu- me, gia- ce la not- te in hor- ri- do sem- bian- te.

Io, ne- mi- co di lu- ce, qual om- bra a- do- lo- ra- ta im- mer- sa nel l'o-

3. Aria

*See critical note for mm. 40–41 and 45–46.

4. Aria

che quest'al- -ma in-ce- ne- rì, con l'ar- dor che tut- to av- vam- -po del mio sen nel tuo par- tir, nel tuo par- -tir, con l'ar- dor che tut- to av- vam- po del mio sen, del mio sen nel tuo par- tir, del mio sen nel tuo par- tir.

5. Aria

Ah! nascondi il tuo rigore o tiranna mia beltà, o tiranna, o tiranna mia beltà! Se quest'alma al fin si more sarà troppa crudeltà. Se quest'alma al fin si mo- re sa- rà tropp- pa cru- del- tà.

Ah! na- scon- di il tuo ri- go- re o tiranna de i- tà, o ti- ran- na, o ti- ran- na de i- tà, o ti- ran- na, o ti- ran- na de i- tà!

6. [Aria]

vuoi ch'io t'a- mi, o va- ga, va- ga, deh! ri- tor- na-mi il cor mi- o, deh! ri-

-tor- na-mi, deh! ri- tor- na-mi il cor mi- o,

che sa- prò con dir- mi ad- di- o, ri- sa- nar

l'ar- den- te pia- ga, l'ar- den- te pia- ga, l'ar- den- te pia-

-ga. Deh! ri- tor- na- mi il cor mi- o, mi- o, se non vuoi ch'io t'a-mi, o va- ga, se non vuo- i, se non vuoi ch'io t'a- -mi, o va- ga, se non vuo- i, se non vuoi ch'io t'a-

7. [Aria]

*See critical note.

32
— con- dan- nò, mi con- dan- nò. Del- l'ar- do- re d'a- mo- re la
40
se- te, del- l'ar- do- re d'a-
48
tr
-mo- re la se- te tut- to, tut- to lie- to io spe- gne- rò,
56
tut- to, tut- to lie- to io
64
spe- gne- rò. Al- le spon- de del- l'on- de di Le- the
71
già Cu- pi- do mi con- dan- nò, mi con- dan- nò,

mi____ con- dan- nò, mi con- dan- nò.

Ritornello

8. Recitativo

Sì, sì, fug- gi cor mi- o d'u- na bel- va cru- del l'hor- ri- do a- spet- to,

ba- si- li- sco in- hu- ma- no, che con sguar- di d'a- mo- re fe- ri- sce l'al- ma

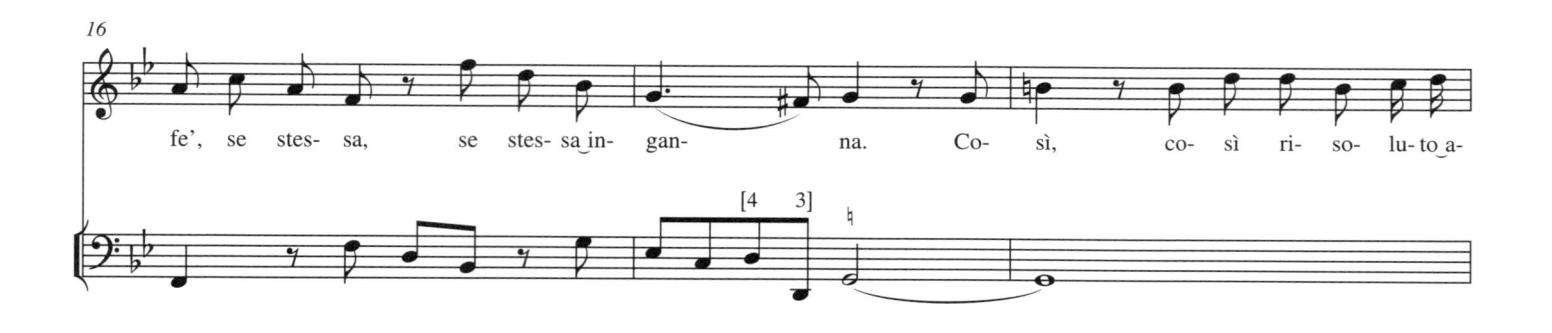

52

et av-ve-le- -na il co- -re. Su! Su! Sde- gno al- la ven- det- ta, al- la ven- -det- ta. Pro- vi, pro- vi que- sta ti- ran- na! Se mi man- ca di fe', se stes- sa, se stes-sa in- gan- na. Co- sì, co- sì ri- so- lu- to a- -mo- re, co- sì con- chiu- do, oh Di- o, ben- ché pia- ga mor- tal re- sti al cor mi- o.

Presto (m. 10)

Adagio recitativo (m. 13)

9. [Aria]

[FINE]

Prima d'esservi infedele
Serenata a voce sola con violini

1. [Introdutione]

Edited by Marie-Louise Catsalis

io mo-ri- rò, mo-ri-rò, mo-ri- rò, lu-ci bel- le,— mo- ri- rò, lu-ci bel- le,— mo-ri- rò.

Fa- ce ar-den- te e stral cru- de- le sol per voi sof-frir sa- prò,_____ fa-ce ar-den- te, stral cru-de- le, sol per voi_ sof- frir sa-prò, sol_ per voi_ sof- frir sa-prò, sof- frir sa- prò.

Pri- ma d'es- ser-vi in- fe- de- le, pri- ma d'es- ser-vi in- fe-

-de- le, lu- ci bel- le, lu- ci bel- le, io mo- ri- rò, mo- ri- rò,

mo- ri- rò, lu- ci bel- le,_ mo- ri- rò, lu- ci bel- le,_ mo- ri- rò.

Largo assai

Du- ri lac- ci, a- spri af- fan- ni, so- no a- tro- ci ti-

-ran- ni a un al- ma a- man - te._

2. Recitativo

Ma se con bella fede, nel penar, nel soffrir, vive costante, perde l'orrido aspetto ogn'empia pena e divien libertà, libertà, e divien libertà, libertà la sua catena. Io, che ancor fui piagata dal crudo stral del pargoletto arciero, piango, sospiro, è vero, ma perché fido è il core, di soave piacere prende grata sembianza il mio do-

3. Aria

ma le stil- le, _____ ma le stil- le _____ che spar- gon gl'al- bo-
e ca- den- do, _____ e ca- den- do _____ dal ci- glio che ge-

-ri, ben- ché fi- glie d'a- cer- bi cor- do- gli, d'a- cer- bi cor- do- gli, so- vra il pra-
-me me- sto pian- to, tri- bu- to d'a- mo- re, tri- bu- to d'a- mo- re, mi nu- tri-

-to nu- tri- sco- no i fio- ri, nu- tri- sco- no i fio- ri, et in- gem- ma-
-sce nel pet- to la spe- me, nel pet- to la spe- me, e m'in- gem- ma-

-no nel ma- re gli sco- gli
-no lo sco- glio del co- re

- gli, _____ nel ma- re gli sco- gli,
- re, _____ lo sco- glio del co- re,

et in- gem- ma- no nel ma- re gli sco-
e m'in- gem- ma- no lo sco- glio del co-

-gli, nel mare gli scogli.
-re, lo scoglio del core.

Ritornello

[Repeat from m. 1 for strophe 2]

4. [Recitativo]

Lie-ta, lie-ta co-sì del-l'a-mor mio ri-man-go, ed è mio preg-gio, e non vil-tà, e non vil-tà, s'io pian-go. Ah, che non è pos-si-bi-le, no, no, no, no, non è pos-si-bi-le ch'io giam-mai ti tra-di-sca, i-do-lo a-ma-to, con ar-di-men-to or-ri-bi-le! S'io ti so-no in-fe-del, m'ol-trag-gi il fa-to: da qual al-tra sa-et-ta e da qual no-do es-ser può l'al-ma mia fe-ri-ta e pre-sa? Co-me, co-me al-tra fiam-ma ac-

Segue

-ce- sa a que-sto cor, si ren-de-rà in-sof-fri- bi- le! Ah, che non è pos--si- bi- le, no, no, no, no, non è pos- si- bi- le!

5. Aria

Andante

Se la sor- te a-ves-se in se-no va-ghe gem-me e rio ve-

-le- no, e_____ l'of- fris- se, e l'of- fris- se, a gl'oc- chi__ mie- i, e l'of- fris- se, a gl'oc- chi__ mie- i,_____ poi di- ces- se: "A- scol- ta_o Clo- ri, a- scol- ta_o Clo- ri, s'al tuo ben_ non sei_ co- stan- te, non sei_ co- stan- te io ti do- no, io ti do- no i miei te- so- ri, i miei te- so- ri, i miei te- -so- ri; ma se tu sei fi- da a- man- te, fi- da a- man- te, il ve- -len lam- bi- sci e mo- ri."

Allegro

Tut- ta lie- ta al- l'hor di- re- i,

tut- ta lie- ta, lie- - - ta al-l'hor di- re- i: "Ric- ca è ve- ro la mer-

-ce- de, ric- ca è ve- ro la mer- ce- de, ma t'in- gan- ni,

t'in- gan- ni, o cie- ca sor- te, o cie- ca sor- te:

Pria ch'of- fen- der la mia fe- de, vo- glio sug- ger la mia mor-

-te, vo- glio sug- ger la mi- a mor- te.

Pria ch'of- fen- der la mia fe- de, vo- glio sug- ger la mia mor-

-te, vo- glio sug- ger la mi- a mor- te, vo- glio

sug- ger la mia mor- - - - - - - - te,

la_ mi- a mor- - - te."

6. Recitativo

Esempio di costanza sarò nel mondo, e s'armi temerario destino contro me con tirannia crudele, ch'ognor costante all'idol mio dirò: "Prima d'esservi infedele, prima d'es- ser-vi in- fe- de- le, lu- ci bel- le, lu- ci bel- le, io mo- ri- rò, mo- ri- rò, mo- ri- rò, lu- ci bel- le, mo- ri- rò, lu- ci bel- le, mo- ri- rò."

FINE

Perché tacete, regolati concenti?
Cantata, alto solo con violini

1. Sinfonia

*See critical note.
Edited by Marie-Louise Catsalis

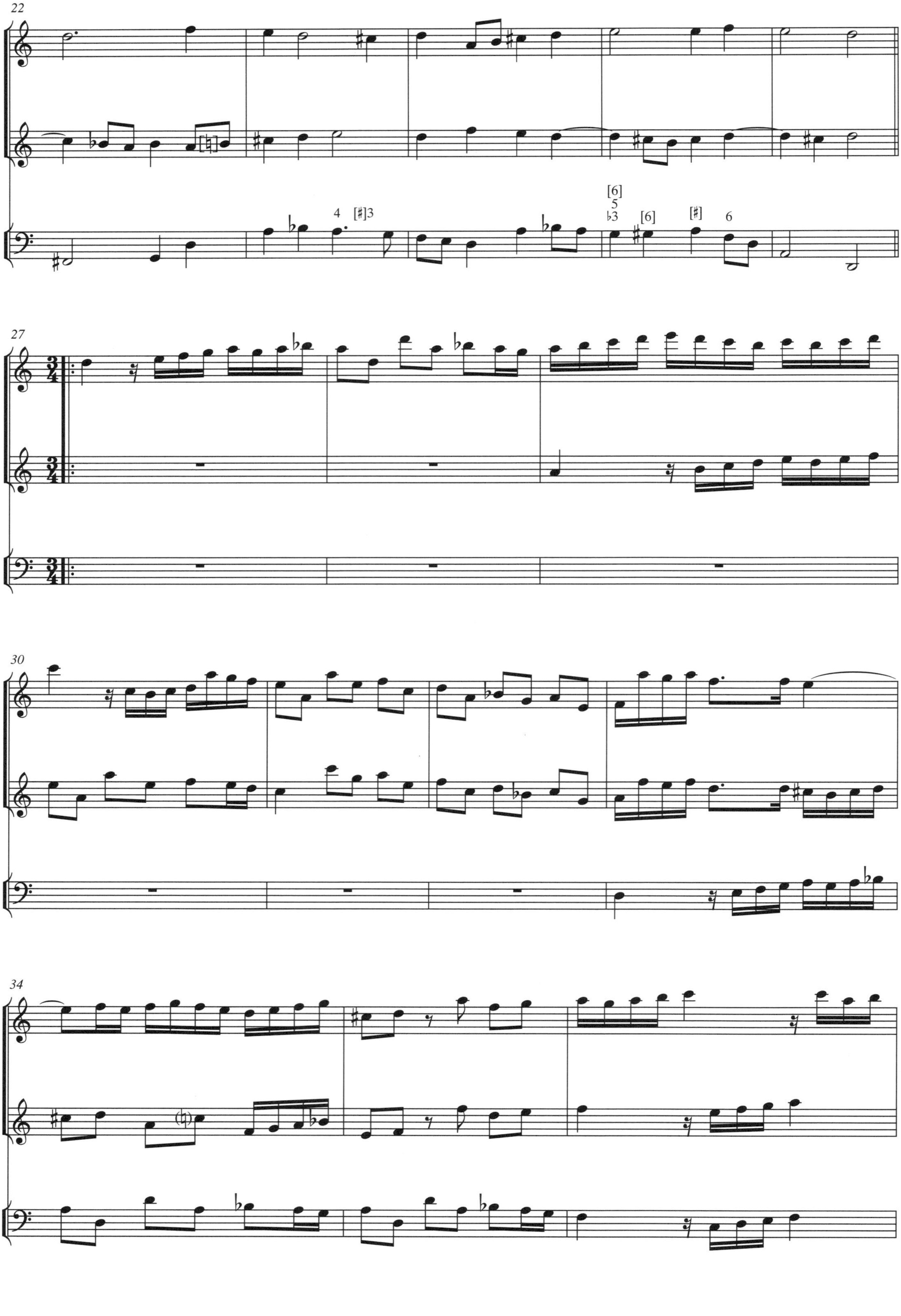
22
4 [♯]3
[6]
5
♭3
[6]
[♯]
6
27
30
34

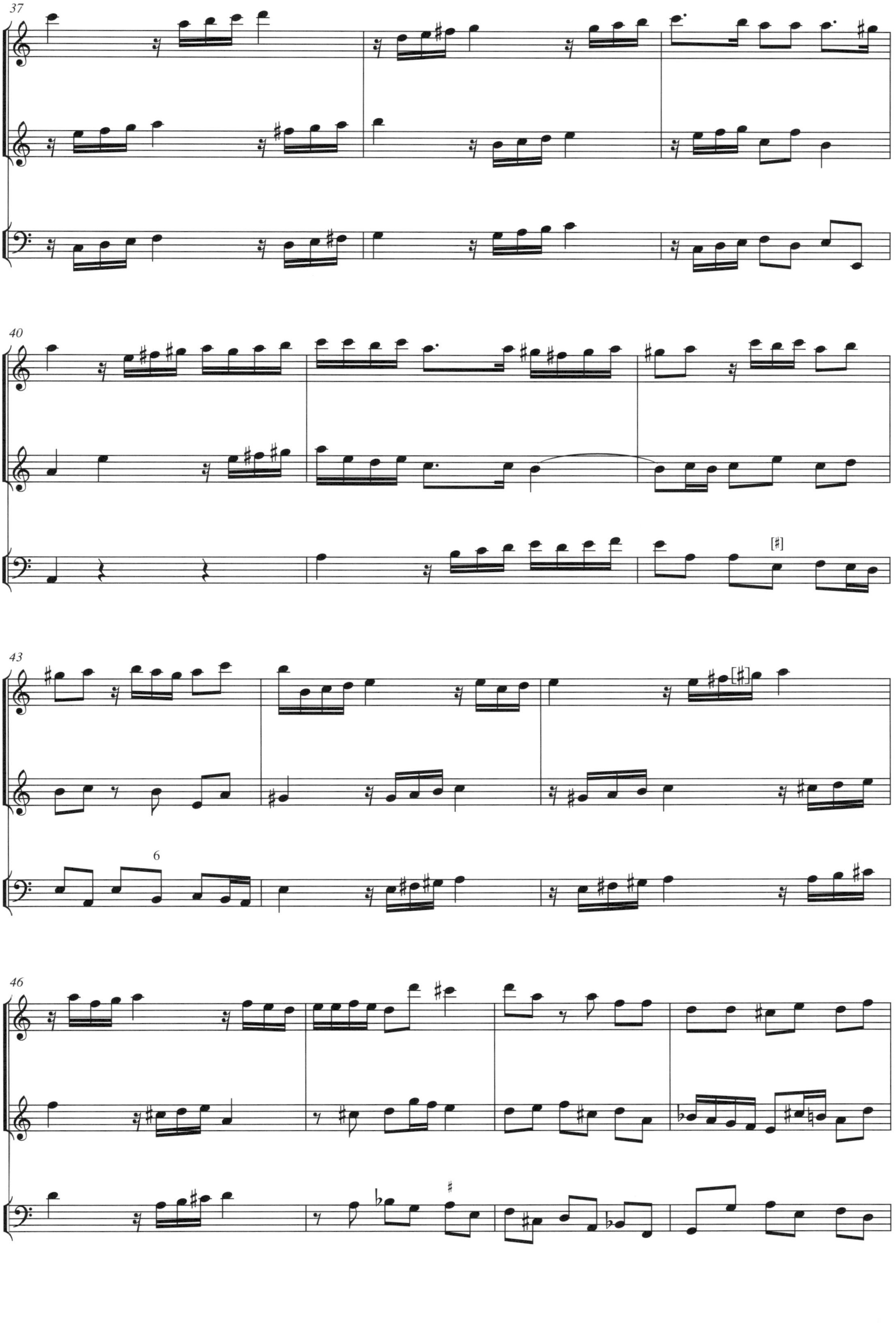
37
40
[♯]
43
6
[♯]
46
♯

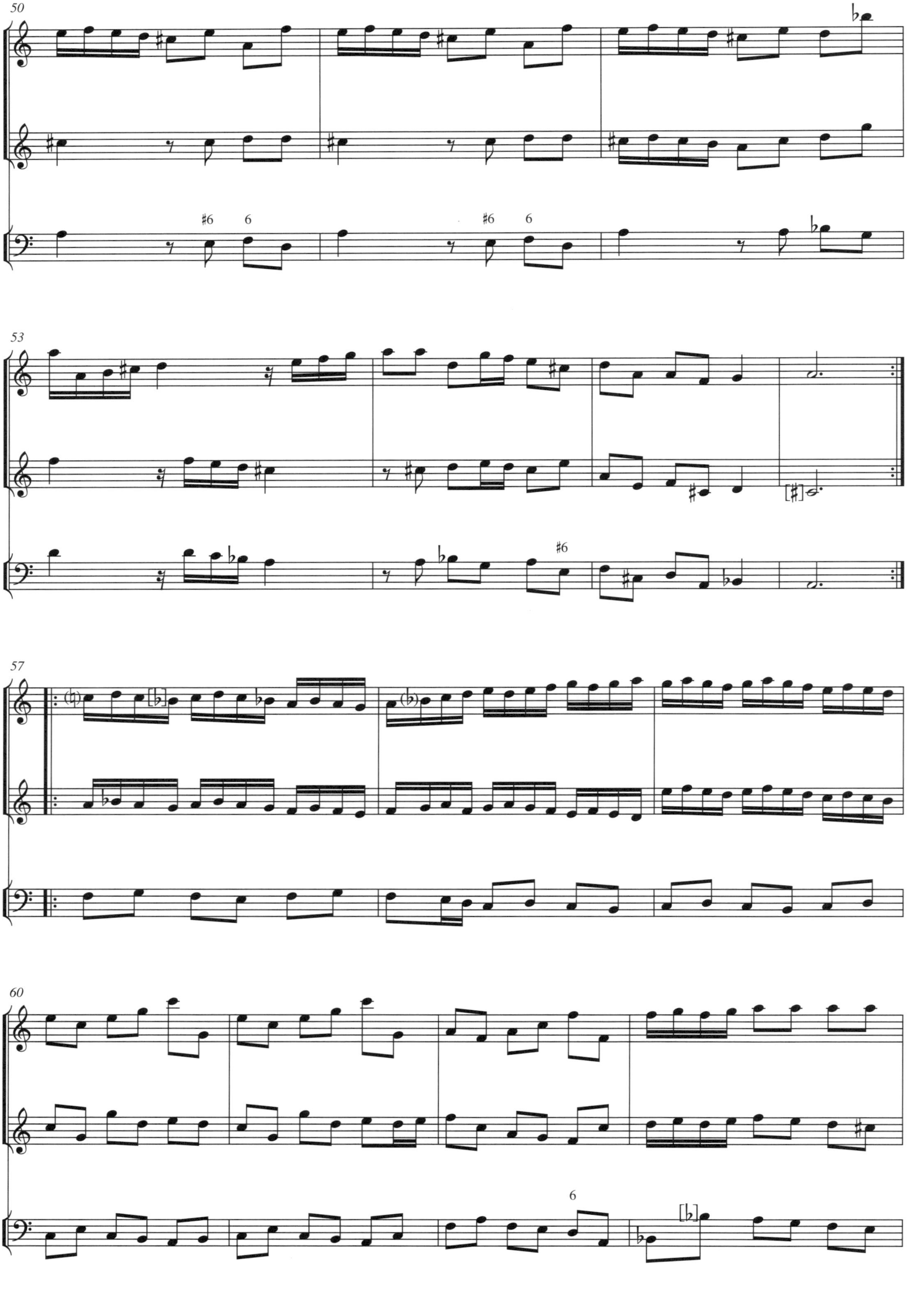
50
#6 6
#6 6
53
#6
57
60
6

77

2. [Recitativo]

Per-ché, per-ché ta-ce- te, re- go- la- ti con- cen- ti? Se- gui- te pur, se- gui- te

3. Aria

1. Al- la ma- no che dot- ta in voi scher- za, quan- to è si- mi- le il Nu- me d'A- mor, al- la
2. Con l'ar- gen- to di guan- cia fio- ri- ta, tes- se i sta- mi a ques- t'al- ma il de- sir, con l'ar-

ma- no che dot- ta in voi scher- - za, quan-to è
-gen- to di guan- cia fio- ri- - ta, tes- se i

si- mi- le il Nu- me d'A- mor, e con l'ar- co d'un ci- glio mi sfer-
sta- mi a que- st'al- ma il de- sir, e al- l'in- vi- to di spe- me gra- di-

-za, et u- ni- sce, u- ni- sce la gio- ia al do-
-ta, cor- ri- spon- de ar- mo- nia, ar- mo- nia di so-

-lor, _____ et u-
-spir, _____ cor- ri-

-ni- sce, u- ni- sce la gio- ia al do- lor.
-spon- de ar- mo- nia, ar- mo- nia di so- spir.

Al- la ma- no _____ che dot- ta in voi scher- - za, quan-to è
Con l'ar- gen- to _____ di guan- cia fio- ri- - ta, tes- se i

si- mi- le il Nu- me d'A- mor, _____ al- la
sta- mi a que- st'al- ma il de- sir, _____ con l'ar-

ma- no che dot- ta in voi scher- za, quan- to è
-gen- to di guan- cia fio- ri- ta, tes- se i

si- mi- le il Nu- me d'A- mor, quan- to è si- mi- le il Nu- me d'A- mor.
sta- mi a que- st'al- ma il de- sir, tes- se i sta- mi a que- st'al- ma il de- sir.

Segue il ritornello

[Ritornello]

5 6 7 6 7 6

6 6 7 6 7 6 ♯6 6

[Repeat from m. 1 for strophe 2]

4. [Recitativo]

Ma che dissi? Tacete! In immagin più bella, vada vivo il tenore di mia sorte rubella. Sì, sì, che del mio ben ne vaghi lumi ha il mio ardore il suo loco. Nè sia stupor che brilli entro i raggi d'un sole il mio bel foco.

5. [Aria]

*See critical note.

1. Tra le fiamme del mio duolo, scenda a volo, scenda a volo
2. Dall'ardor dei tuoi bei lumi, si consumi, si consumi,

un sol rag-gio di tu-a bel-tà. E sa-
fred-do gel che mi ser-pe nel sen. E 'l ba-

-rà la bel-l'i-ri-de_al mi-o co-ghie-re, quel l'ar-
-len d'un tuo sguar-do lu-sin-ghie-ro sia fo-

-do-rie-ro ch'a-spra guer-ra, a spra guer-ra nel pet-to mi fa.
-ren a que-st'al-ma, a que-st'al-ma d'un gior-no se-ren.

E__ sa- rà la bel- l'i- ri- de al mi- o co- ghie- re,
E 'l__ ba- len d'un tuo sguar- do lu- sin- ghie- ro

quel l'ar- do- re ch'a- spra guer- ra, a- spra guer- ra nel pet- to mi
sia__ fo- rie- ro a que- st'al- ma, a__ que- st'al- ma d'un gior- no se-

fa.
-ren. Tra__ le fiam- me del__
Dal- l'ar- dor dei tuoi__

[Repeat from m. 1 for strophe 2]

6. [Recitativo]

Nè m'ascolti, crudele, così le tue vittorie o non curi o disprezzi. Scopri del tuo poter le forze homai fia ch'ogni orror disgombre. Farai nascer il giorno, in mezzo al l'ombre. Ah, che ben io v'intendo, stelle d'amor nemiche. Per tormentare i miei pensieri amanti volete anco sprezzare i propri vanti.

7. [Aria]

Largo

1. Dor- mi, dor- mi, ma sap- pi al- men che_____ per te_____ mo- ro,_____ che_____ per te_____ mo- ro. E al dol- ce tuo so- por en- -tro di que- sto sen, ve- glia il mar- to- ro, ve- glia il mar- to- ro. E al dol- ce tuo so- por en-

2. Dor- mi, dor- mi, ch'il mio do- lor ne- nia al tuo_____ son- no,_____ ne- nia al tuo son- no. For- se ne' so- gni an- cor, cru- da, ti sa- prò dir: "Te so- la a- do- ro, te so- la a- do- ro." For- se ne' so- gni an- cor, cru-

-tro di que- sto sen, ve- glia il mar- to- ro, ve- glia il mar-
-da, ti sa- prò dir: "Te so- la a- do- ro, te so- la a-

-to- ro, il mar- to- ro.
-do- ro, a- do- ro."

Dor- mi, dor- mi, ma sap- pi al- men che
Dor- mi, dor- mi, ma sap- pi al- men che

per te mo- ro, che
per te mo- ro, che

per te mo- ro, mo- ro.
per te mo- ro, mo- ro.

[Segue il ritornello]

Ritornello

[Repeat from m. 1 for strophe 2]

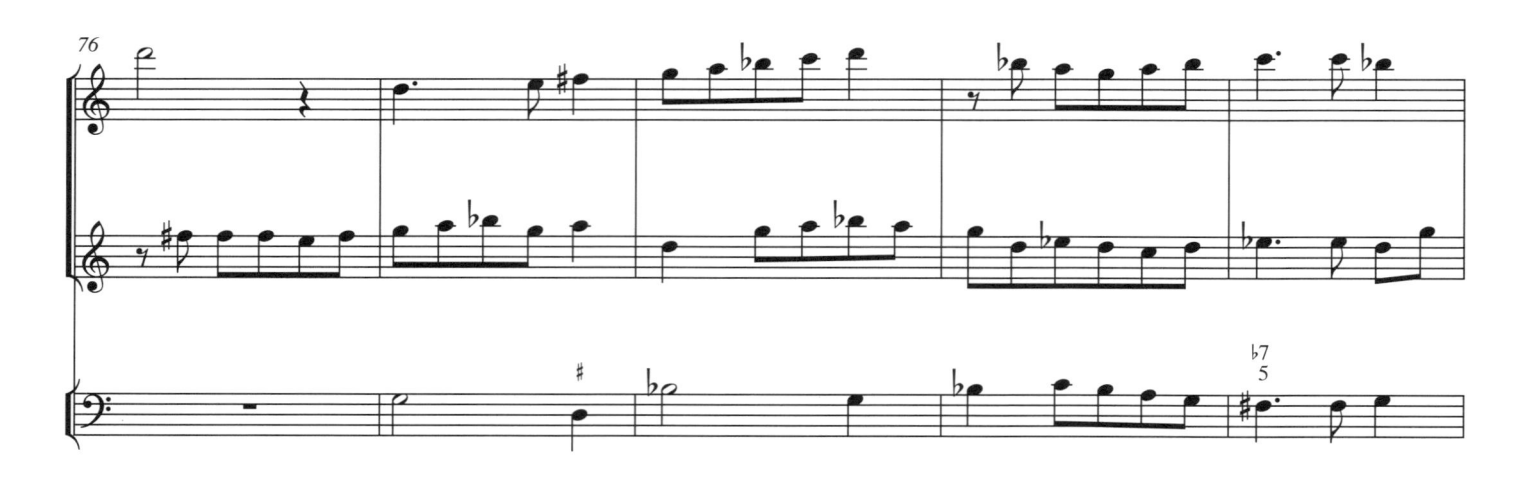

8. [Recitativo]

Ma ti- ran- na, tu dor- mi e tra le so- po- ri o Di- o,

non puoi nè vuoi u- di- re il pian- - - - to mi- o.

9. [Aria]

1. Deh pen- sie- ri in me si schie- ri a bat- ta- glia, a bat-
2. Se ri- po- so io più non o- so a do- man- da- re, do- man-

-ta- - - - glia, il fie- ro, il fie- ro
-da- - - re, il Di- o, il Dio d'A-

[6 ♭5] [6] [♭] [♯]

stuol. Et as- sa- — gli-a il du- ro co- re, et as- sa-
-mor, col de- sta- — re, chi m'in- pia- — ga, col de- sta-

-glia il du- ro co- re che l'ar- do- — re del mio a- mor sen- tir non
-re, chi m'in- pia- — ga la mia pia- ga pro- ve- rà men cru- do il

vuol, _____ che l'ar- do- — re del mio a- mor sen- tir non vuol.
duol, _____ la mia pia- ga pro- ve- rà men cru- do il duol.

93

Sotto l'ombra d'un faggio
Serenata a voce sola con violini
1. [Introdutione]

Edited by Marie-Louise Catsalis

Sot- to l'om- bra d'un fag- gio, sul mar- gi- ne d'un ri- vo in brac- cio al son- no, sta- va Fi- le- no, ab- ban- do- na- to e so- lo. Quan- do scos- so dal duo- lo, par che ha-ve- a so- gna- to d'es-ser in-ca- te- na- to. Bal-zò da ter- ra, e co- me al-cun l'u- dis- se,

ad oc- chi chiu-si al- zò le vo- ci, ad oc- chi chiu-si al- zò le

vo- ci e dis- se:

Segue

*See critical note.

2. Aria

Scio- glie- te- mi, la- scia- te- mi, ch'è trop- po cru- del- tà, è trop- po cru- del- tà. Scio- glie- te- mi, la- -scia- te- mi, scio- glie- te- mi, la- scia- te- mi, ch'è trop- po cru- del- tà, è trop- po cru- del- tà, è trop- po cru- del- tà. Ren-

[Fine–Ritornello]

99

-de- te- mi, do- na- te- mi la ca- ra li- ber- tà, la ca- ra li- ber-

-tà. Ren- de- te- mi, do- na- te- mi la ca- ra li- ber- tà, la ca- ra, ca- ra, ca-

-ra, ren- de- te- mi, do- na- te- mi la ca- ra li- ber- tà.

[Dal segno al fine]

Ritornello

Segue

3. Recitativo

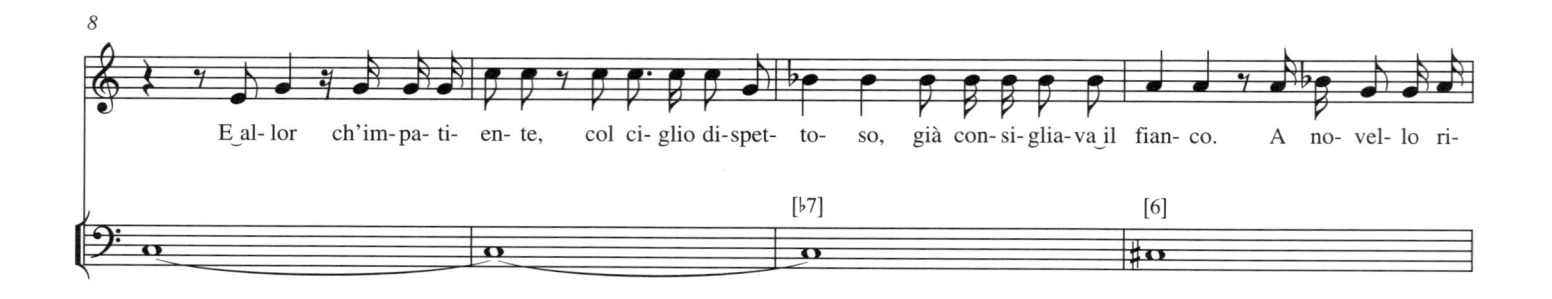

Pietà, pietà lasciate! Ei replicar volea, ma gl'occhi aprendo, e scorto ch'al ruscello alle piante egli parlava, s'avvide che sognava. E allor ch'impaziente, col ciglio dispettoso, già consigliava il fianco. A novello riposo, vide Filli la vaga e non fu sogno. Onde, ver lei movendo ben frettoloso il passo, persuadeva così quel cor di sasso:

Segue l'aria à violino solo

4. Aria

Io dor- mi- vo pres- so al ri- vo,

io dor- mi- vo pres- so al ri- vo e so- gna- i, ma non er- -rai, che m'ha- ve- a- no in- ca- te- na- to men- tre son vi- ci- no a te! Io dor- mi- vo pres- so al ri- vo e so- gna- i, ma non er- ra- i, che m'ha-

-vea-no in-ca- te- na-to, in-ca- te- na- to men-tre son__ vi- ci- no a te,

che m'ha- vea-no in-ca- te- na-to, in-ca- te- na- to men- tre son__

vi- ci- no a te! Ha ra-

Fine
Segue [il ritornello]

-gio-ne il mi- o co- re in-na-mo- ra- to, il mio co-re in-na- mo- ra-to, ha ra-

*The ritornello may begin at m. 56.

-gio- ne ch'è pri- gio- ne del- la fe'. Ha ra- gio- ne il mio co- -re, il mio co- re in- na- mo- ra- to, ha ra- gio- ne ch'è pri- gio- ne del- la fe', ch'è pri- gio- ne del- la fe'. Io dor-

Dal segno al fine

Ritornello

5. Recitativo

Ragione, ragione ha il cor, ma il labro non ha ragion. Se esclama, per haver libertade, e star disciolto su l'altar del tuo volto, i delirii del labro, o bella, io sveno; e se giammai ricuserà d'amarti, per reo, per reo dichiaro il seno.

6. Aria

Tal- vol- ta il do- lo- re, che d'es- ser fe- li- ce non cre- de al- la spe- me, si sen- te sul la- bro chia- mar li- ber- tà, si sen- te sul la- bro chia- mar li- ber- tà, li- ber- tà, li- ber- tà.

Talvolta il dolore, che d'esser felice non crede alla speme, si sente sul labro chiamar libertà, chiamar libertà, libertà, libertà, libertà, libertà. Che fugga le pene del regno d'amore, il labro lo dice, il labro lo dice, ma il cor, ma il cor non lo sa, _non lo sa, ma il cor_____ non_____ lo sa, no, no, non lo sa. Che fug- ga le pe- ne del re- gno d'a- mo- re, il la- bro lo di- ce, il la- bro lo di- ce, ma il cor non lo sa, non lo sa, ma il cor non lo sa, ma il cor_____ non_____ lo sa, no, no, non lo sa, no, no, non lo sa.

FINE

Notte, ch'in carro d'ombre
Serenata, soprano solo con violini

1. [Introdutione]

Edited by Rosalind Halton

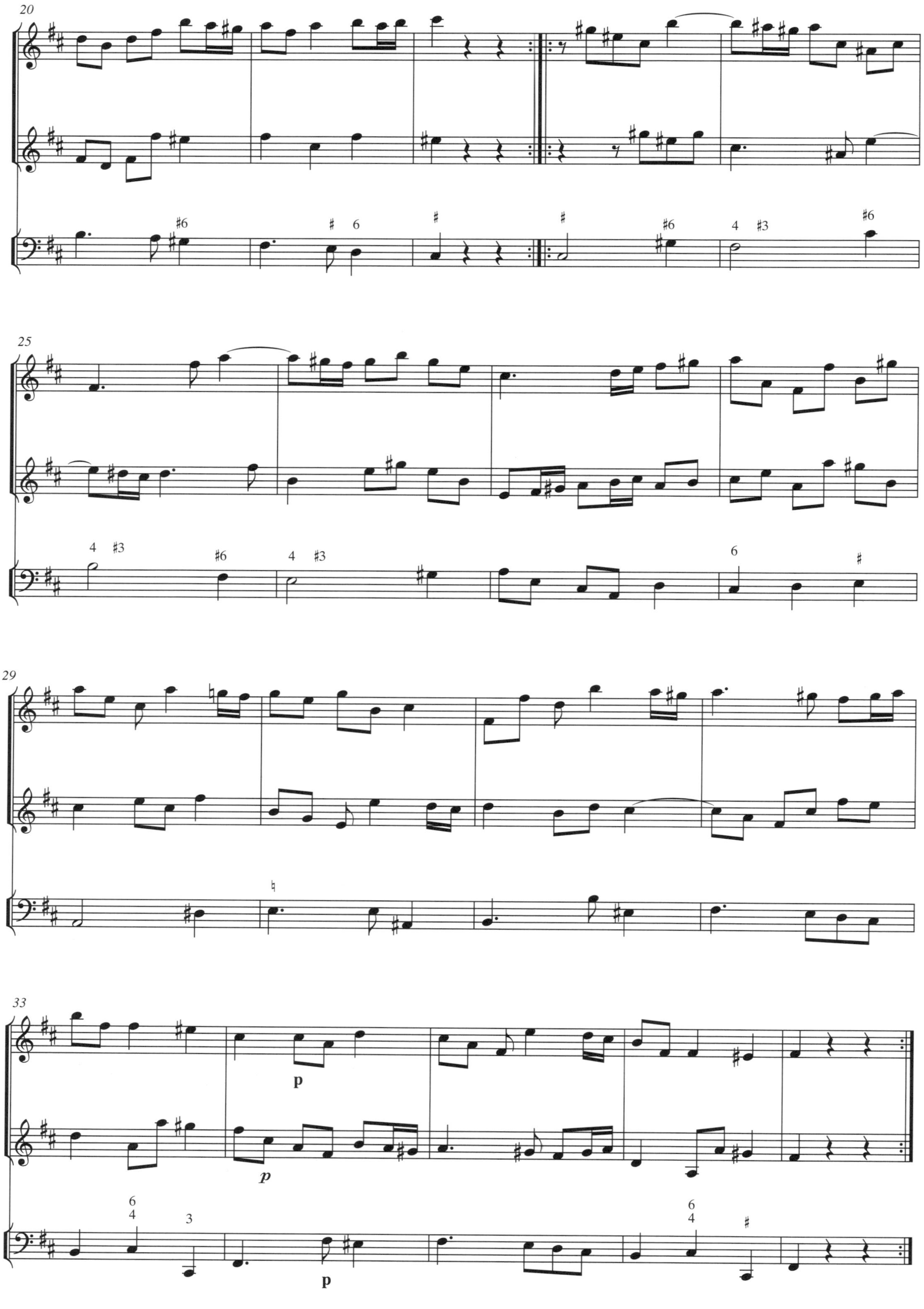
20
25
29
33
p
p
p

2. [Recitativo]

Notte, ch'in carro d'ombre per l'a-e-rei sen-tier rag-gi-ri il cor-so, ve-lo-ce ol-tre l'u-sa-to con la sfer-za di stel-le a' tuoi bru-ni de-strier fla-gel-

112

-li il dor- so. E ral- len- ta- to il mor- so mentre ra- pi- da scor- ri en- tro l'e- te- re[a] mo- le, gui- da- mi, gui- da- mi, o ca- ra Not- te, in grem- bo al so- le.

3. [Aria]

Largo e piano

Vie- ni, o Not- te, vie- ni, o Not- te, e in questo petto faccian tregua i rei martiri.

Notte, vieni, vieni, o Notte e in questo petto faccian tregua i rei martiri, faccian tregua i rei martiri, i rei martiri.

36
1. [to m. 41]
2.
E sian
5 6
[Fine]
41
gui- da al ca- ro og- get- to, al ca- ro og- get- to l'au- re
45
sol de' miei so- spi- ri, sian gui- da al ca- ro og-
6 4 ♯3 6

-get-to, al ca- ro og-get-to l'au- re sol de' miei so- spi- ri, de' miei so-spi- - - ri.

[Dal segno al fine]

4. [Recitativo]

E tu, ch'o-gnor ti van-ti fug-gir sen-za ri-tor- no e de' pro-prii tuoi par-ti es-ser ti-ran- no, in-gra-tis-si-mo Tem-po, per-ché non to-gli un an-no di pe- ne a

5. [Aria]

Allegro

118

sol, fug- ge e di- le- gua- si il gior- no e 'l sol. sol.

Fine

Per

es- ser fie- re con- tro il mio co- re, si fer- man l'o- re,

po- san le sfe- re sol per mio duol. Per es- ser fie- re

contro il mio core, si fer- man l'o- re,

po- san le sfe- re, contro il mio co- re,

sol per mio duol, _____ sol per mio duol.

[Dal segno al fine]

6. Recitativo

Ma parmi ch'e-sau-di-te renda le mie pre-ghie-re, e con o-scuro vel Notte pieto-sa invita o-gni mor-ta-le a pren-der po-sa. Dor-mi, dor-mi, A-ma-ril-li, sol ve-gli questo co-re o-ve scolpì di Tir-si la bel-la i-ma-go A-mo-re. E so-gni l'al-ma a-man-te quei pia-cer, quei di-let-ti, che go-de-re non può fuor del ri-po-so. Quin-di tac-cia-no in-tan-to i miei so-spi-ri e 'l mor- mo- ri-   o del pian- to.

7. [Aria]

Adagio (Largo)

123

*See the editorial methods, penultimate paragraph.
†See critical note on notation of dotted rhythms.

124

dol- ce, dol- ce son- no, son-no dol- ce, dol-ce son- no, son-no dol-ce, vie- ni a me,

dol- ce, dol- ce son- no, son-no dol- ce, dol-ce son- no, son-no dol-ce, vie- ni a

me.

[Fine]

E con l'ombra sì gradita del mio sol, della mia vita, dona tregua al mio martire, lusingando la mia fe'. E con l'ombra sì gradita del mio sol, della mia vita, dona tregua al mio martire, lusingan- - do, lusin-

126

-gan- do la mia fe'. Con l'i-

[Dal segno al fine]

8. [Recitativo]

Ma voi non vi chiu- de- te, mie do- len- ti pu- pil- le? Ohi- mè, che fia?

Ah' ben l'in- ten- do, sì: l'a- ni- ma mi- a so- lo av- vez- za ai mar- ti- ri, non co- no- sce ri-

-po- so. Sì, sì, ve- glia Amaril- li, e i tuoi so- spi- ri se tre- gua a- ver non pon- no,

9. [Aria]

Allegrissimo
[Violini all'unisoni]

Sì, sì____ che pri- va di con- ten- to, che

pri- va di con-ten- to, go- de- rò, go- de- rò del

mio mo- rir, go- de- rò, go- de- rò del mio mo- rir. Sì, sì che pri- va di con-

-ten- to, go- de- rò, go- de- rò del mio mo-

-rir, goderò, goderò del mio mo-

-rir, goderò del mio morir.

[Fine]

Se goder non posso in vita la cagion del mio tormento, sol la morte mi è gradita come fi- - ne, come fi- ne al mio mar- tir. Se go- der non pos- so in vi- ta la ca- gion del mio tor- men- to, sol la mor- te mi è gra- di- ta come fine al mio martir, come fi- -ne al mio mar- tir.

FINE

[Dal segno al fine]

Hor che di Febo ascosi
Serenata, soprano solo con violini

1. Introdutione

2. Recitativo

Hor che di Febo a- sco- si stan- no in sen d'An- fi- tri- te i rai splen- den- ti, non fia stu- por se ne- gl'al- trui ri- po- si con so- no- ri con- cen- ti vo tem- pran- do il mio duo- lo, ch'è pro- prio de- gl'a- -man- ti fra so- li- ta- ri- i or- ro- ri spie- gar del co- re i più se- cre- ti a- mo- ri.

3. Aria

Grave e piano

Ca- ra,_____ ca- ra, ca- ra not- te,

che i fur- ti gio- con- di de- gl'a- man- ti be- ni- gna ri- co- pri.

Ca- ra, ca- ra not- te, ca- ra, ca- ra not- te, che i fur- ti gio-

-con- di de- gl'a- man- ti be- ni- gna ri- co-

136

Ben puoi__ tu [Fine]

quei di- let- ti ch'a- scon- di nu- me- rar con le stel- le che sco-

-pri. Ben puoi tu quei di- let- ti ch'a- -scon- di nu- me- rar con le stel- le che sco- -pri, con le stel- le che sco-

4. Recitativo

Ma chim'ad-di-ta, o Di-o, del bel-l'i-do-lo mi-o fra que-st'om-bre not--tur-ne il vi-so a-dor-no? Voi sol po-te-te il gior-no re-car se vi de-sta-te, oc-chi, oc-chi ri-den-ti, s'ha-ve-te e-gua-le al sole i rag-gi ar-den-ti.

*(ha-ve-te e-gual--men-te)

Siegue

*Text underlay variant from D-MÜs.

5. Aria

-pil- le a- mo- ro- se. -pil- le a- mo- ro- se.

[Fine–Ritornello]

Ch'il vo- stro splen- do- re

dà vi- ta a que- st'al- ma e bru- gia il mio

co- re con fa- ci gra- di- te, con fiam- me di ro- se, con fiam- me, con

fiam- me di ro- se. Ch'il vo- stro splen- do- re

dà vi- ta a que- st'al- ma e bru- gia il mio

co- re___ con fa- ci gra- di- te, con fiam- me, con fiam- me di ro- se, con fiam- me di ro- se.

[Dal segno] subito

Ritornello

6. Recitativo

Quin- di dai vo- stri sguar- di il mio mar- to- ro

Largo

go- de in mez- zo ai so- spir dol- ce ri- sto- ro, go- de in mez- zo ai so- spir dol- ce ri- sto-

Siegue aria con violini

7. Aria

A tempo lento

Va- go fior,

vago fior,_____ ch'in not-te al-gen-te_____ lan- guir fred- -do, lan- guir fred- do in ter- ra_____ suo- le,

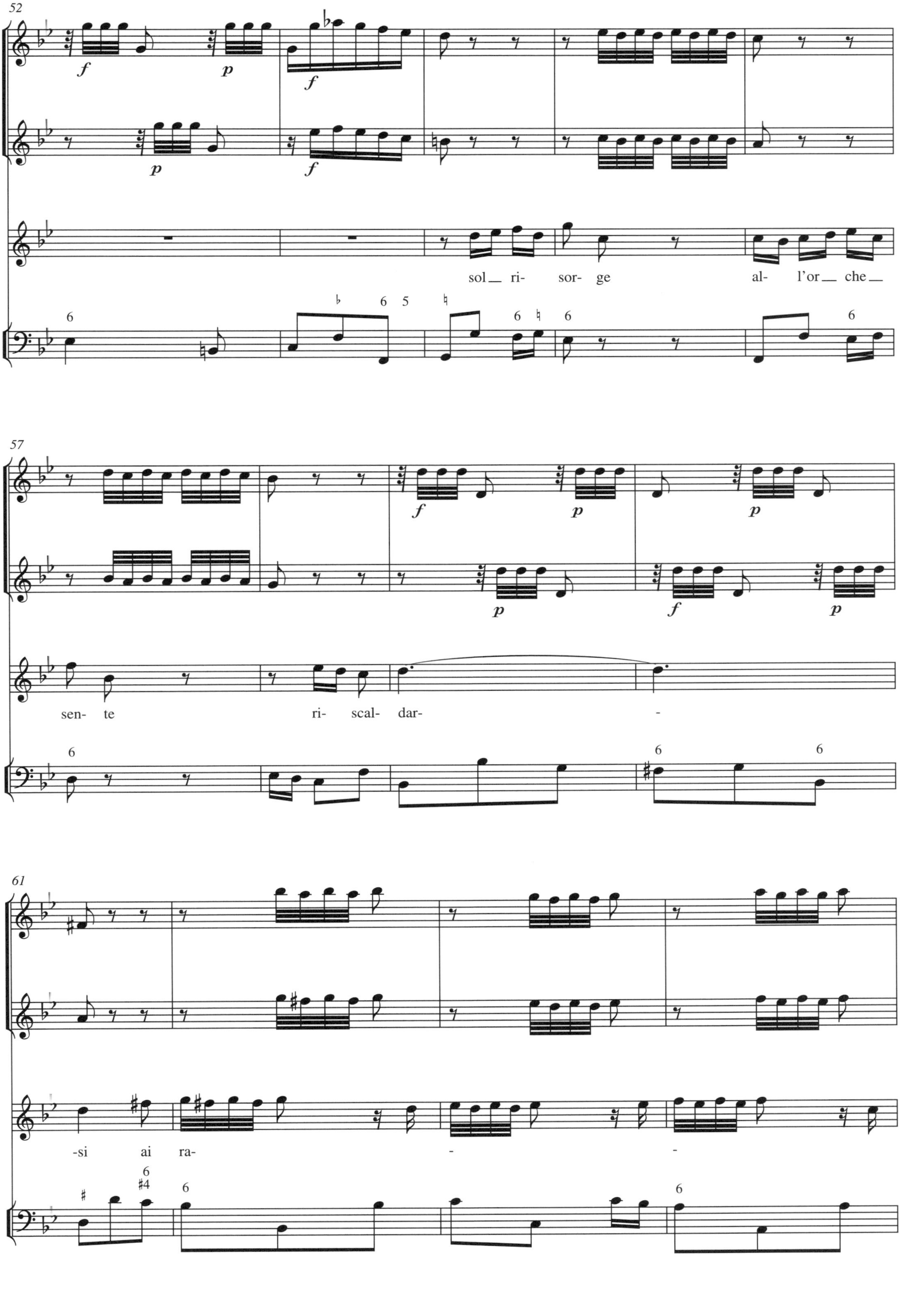
52
sol_ ri- sor- ge al- l'or_ che_
57
sen- te ri- scal- dar- -
61
-si ai ra- - -

i del so- le, sol ri- sor- ge al- l'or che sen- te

ri- scal- dar - si ai ra - - - i del so- le, ai ra - - i

8. Recitativo

Ma no, riposa_o bella, ch'an-che dor-men-do a-scol-te-rai mie pe-ne, e fra not-tur-ne sce-ne con ac-ce-sa fa-vel-la, sa-prà mo-strar-ti il mio tra-fit-to co-re, di-ve-nu-to fan-ta-sma il Dio, il Dio d'A-mo-re.

9. Aria

Dor- mi- te, po- sa-

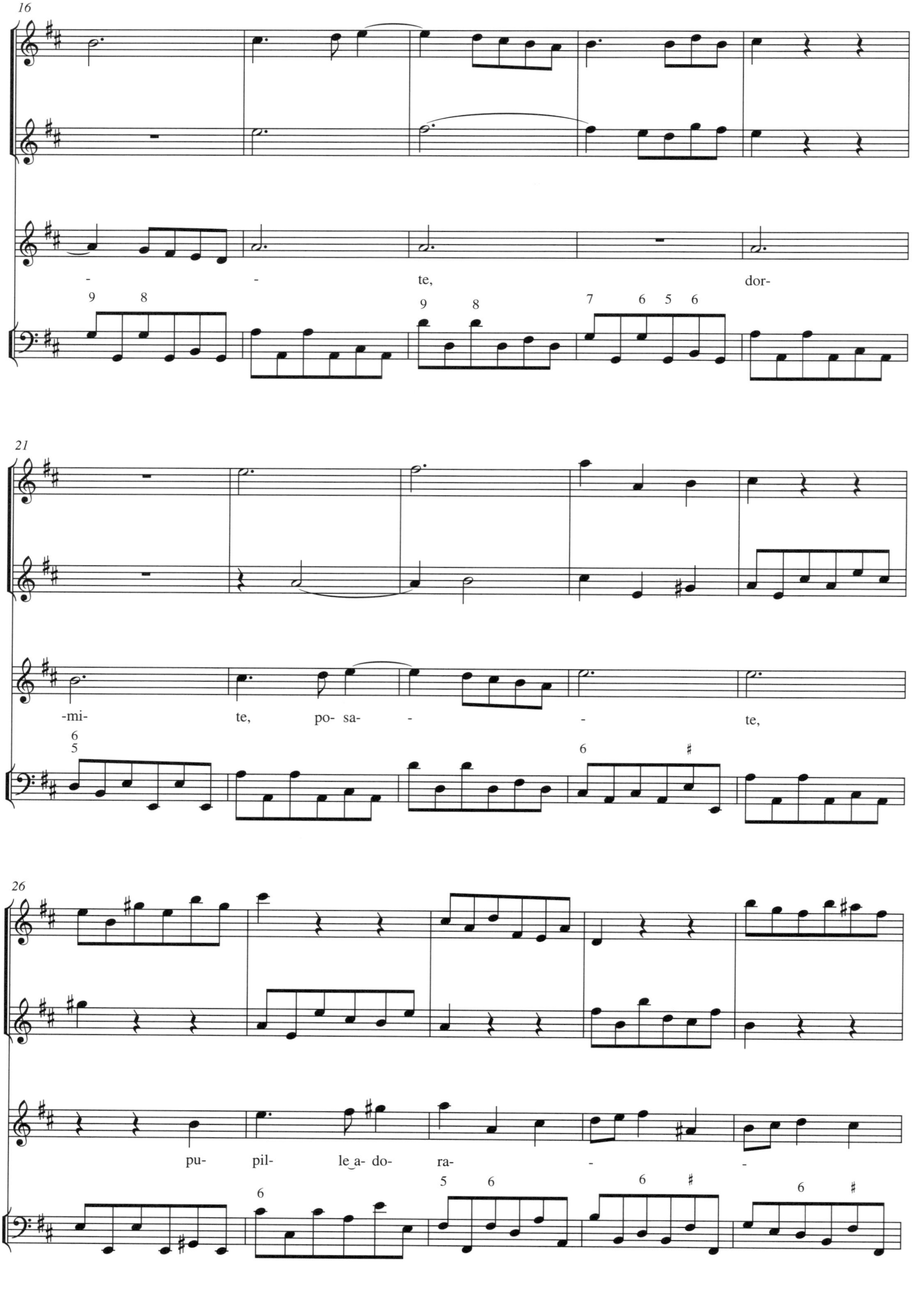
16
- - te, dor-
21
-mi- te, po- sa- - - te,
26
pu- pil- le a- do- ra- - -

-te, pu- pil- le_a- do- ra- - te, in pla- ci- do_o- bli- o. Dor- -ma, dor- ma_il vo- stro splen- dor, dor- ma_il vo- stro splen- dor ch'io parto, dor- ma il vo- stro splen- dor ch'io par-

-to. Ad- di- o, ad- di- o.

FINE

Critical Report

Sources

Sventurati miei penzieri (H. 710)

There is one extant source:

> Parma, Conservatorio di Musica A. Boito (I-PAc), Sanv. B.1/CF-VI-44. Watermark: three crescents. Title information: "Serenata | A voce sola di Canto | Del Sigr. Alessandro Scarlata | Al'uso del Sigr. | D. Benedetto Tedeschi." Copyist: unknown hand.

The watermark of three crescents in a single circle indicates Venetian provenance, perhaps an early connection to Scarlatti's influential patron of Venetian origin, Cardinal Pietro Ottoboni. This single-work manuscript is bound together in a collection entitled "Cantate di Eccellenti Autori," which includes Domenico Valentini, Nicolò Porpora, Benedetto Marcello, Domenico Scarlatti, Baron d'Astorja, and Sigr. Sasone (with Hasse added in pencil).

Hanley notes that the spelling of Scarlatti using an earlier form of the name (i.e., Scarlata) indicates that *Sventurati miei penzieri* is most likely one of the earliest examples of Scarlatti's vocal writing.[1] There are other indications of the early date of this work. For example, the basso continuo figuring places a sharp or flat in front of the bass note, rather than the more common later practice of placing the figure below or above the staff (often on the space or line required), so that at first reading it may look like an accidental. The use of accidentals also follows an older practice of being placed before every note in the bar and is often not cancelled by a natural even when modern practice would require it.

Sventurati miei penzieri is one of two Scarlatti serenatas that does not have obbligato instruments. According to Neapolitan practice, this was an early form of the serenata genre seen in the 1660s through the 1680s.[2] Unlike many vocal works of this time, it does not open with a recitative, and there is no instrumental introduction. Not even a single chord precedes the entry of the voice, which calls for the practice of an improvized introduction, as exemplified by Scarlatti's *Varie introduzzioni per mettersi in tono delle compositioni* (GB-Lbl 14424). As was the practice in the late seventeenth century, this work is in one continuous movement, with frequent changes in meter and tempo, including short arioso sections, instead of clear delineation of recitative and aria. Rather, the work gradually takes form, ending with a strophic aria in two verses that uses an ostinato rhythm with obsessive phrases reminiscent of a ground bass. The serenata is in the key of C minor, notated with a key signature of one flat, based within the three-flat hexachord on C. It is a common key of Scarlatti's solo serenatas, which may well follow the example set by earlier Neapolitan composers of the solo serenata genre (e.g., Simona Coya and Giovanni Cesare Netti). Indeed, many of the early works of this genre, as identified by Fabris, make use of this dark key. It is used in many of Scarlatti's works now known as cantatas (perhaps undesignated serenatas?) with night themes.

Eurilla, amata Eurilla (H. 252)

The number of extant manuscripts attests to the popularity of this work. *Eurilla, amata Eurilla* exists today in seven sources, as listed below in their order of importance. An eighth copy is listed in Hanley as being an uncatalogued manuscript held in the Sächsische Landesbibliothek, Dresden; however the library reports this copy as missing.[3]

> A) Naples, Conservatorio di Musica San Pietro a Majella (I-Nc), Ms. 34.5.19, fols. 24v–28r. Watermark: fleur-de-lys in a double circle, then later a quadruped in a single circle. Title information: "Eurilla amata Eurilla: | Serenata a voce sola | Del Sigr. Alessandro Scarlatti [Scarlatti crossed out and 'Stradella' added in library hand]." Copyist: Naples, Scribe B; this copyist is often seen in the cantatas of Scarlatti and in particular the works in this volume of solo serenatas; the scribe can also be identified in opera manuscripts, including *Giasone* of Cavalli (I-Nc, Ms. 33.6.15) and *Argia* of Cesti (I-Nc, Ms. 33.6.12).[4]

> B) Paris, Bibliothèque nationale de France (F-Pn), D11840/FG10502, fols. 143r–150r. Watermark: fleur-de-lys in a single circle. Title information: "Eurilla amata Eurilla | Serenata a Voce Sola | Del Sig. Alessandro | Scarlatti." No. 9 in a collection of ten vocal works by Alessandro Scarlatti. Copyist: Naples, Scribe B (see source A above).

> C) Conservatoire royal de Bruxelles (B-Bc), F670, page numbers added, pp. 65–72. Watermark: three crescents, of Venetian origin.[5] No title information. Copyist: unknown hand.

> D) London, British Library (GB-Lbl), Add. 31518, fols. 27r–30r; page numbers added, pp. 53–59. Watermark not legible. No title information.

E) London, Royal College of Music (GB-Lcm), 1101 (examined only as a reproduction), fols. 5r–7r. Title information (attribution only): "Del S. Alessandro Scarlatti." Copyist: William Croft, 1697.[6]

F) Museo internazionale e biblioteca della musica di Bologna (I-Bc), V279 (consulted only at library), fols. 84v–96v. Watermark: fleur-de-lys in a double circle. No title information. The manuscript is 8.5 × 21cm, with only one system per page, in a collection of cantatas by Scarlatti, Alessandro Stradella, Severo de Luca, and Bernardo Pasquini. Copyist: unknown hand.

G) London, Royal College of Music (GB-Lcm), 581 (examined only as a reproduction), fols. 75r–80r. Title information: "Cantata a Voce Sola | Del Sig.r Alessandro | Scarlatti." The copy is signed "Francesco Vitale, sono servitore," likely the scribe, and it is likely a copy of source A or B above.

As would be expected given so many sources, there are many variations between the scores, not least of which is the incipit. Hanley gives the following variation of the incipit, which he states is common to manuscripts C, E, and F:

Eurilla, amata Eurilla is the second of the two Scarlatti serenatas (indicated by title) that do not make use of instrumental obbligato lines. Scored for one voice and basso continuo, this work resembles more the renaissance lute serenade. Moreover, the text is sung by the forlorn lover, anguished at his imminent departure from the object of his affections. In common with the serenata genre, the text is connected with the night—a time for intimate revelations of the soul. The work ends with a recitative that announces the sunrise, significant because it heralds the moment of departure. This forms a part of the very widespread textual topos that has been described as "lovers' meetings and partings at dawn."[7]

All'hor che stanco il sole (H. 33)

There is one extant source:

Paris, Bibliothèque nationale de France (F-Pn), D.11841, fols. 227r–254r. Watermark: shield of a running man with a cross.[8] Title information: "Serenata a Voce Sola." Copyist: Naples, Scribe B (see *Eurilla, amata Eurilla*, source A).

This serenata exists in a volume containing sixteen vocal works, several by Alessandro Scarlatti, for example, the duet cantata *Clori e Lisa* (28 February 1706) and solo cantata *Nel dolce tempo* (29 May 1712); also a Cleopatra cantata attributed to his son Domenico, a duet *Questo silenzio* by Antonio Pistocco [Pistocchi], and works by unidentified composers. The catalogue includes the note of a librarian ("M. R. Meylan, June 8, '55") that this volume was copied from manuscripts in the library of the conservatory at Naples.

The scribe identified by Amato as Scribe B is regarded by him as one of a small group of copyists active in Naples in the 1670s and 1680s.[9] It is therefore appropriate that this scribe associated with Scarlatti's earlier career should be the most frequent to appear in this collection of *Serenate a voce sola*, given that it too is a genre more at home in the seventeenth century. Apart from *All'hor che stanco il sole*, Scribe B is the hand of two copies of *Eurilla, amata Eurilla*, two copies of *Prima d'esservi infedele*, and one copy of *Sotto l'ombra d'un faggio*.

It is not surprising that this scribe's musical notation adheres to conventions of the seventeenth century, which today challenge readers more at home with modern conventions. For example, regarding accidentals, once the accidental has been indicated, it is assumed that it is retained for the entire passage or until cancelled, especially when other accidentals in the sequence are added. For example, B-flat and E-flat may be indicated several bars earlier than an A-flat, but the presence of the A-flat indicates that the accidentals are cumulative, therefore it is inclusive of the B-flat and E-flat. Likewise with basso continuo figures, often a sharp or flat indicating the quality of the interval of a third will be placed beside the note and on its respective line or space, instead of below or above the note. Beaming is erratic, or perhaps better, inventive. It can be an indication of a type of articulation to be played, though not to the exclusion of other possible articulations, as the notation is not consistent, and also can suggest the rate of harmonic change to the continuo player.

Hor che l'aurato nume (H. 516)

There is one extant source:

Paris, Bibliothèque nationale de France (F-Pn), Vm7 61bis, fols. 55r–62r. Watermarks alternate between a bunch of grapes and block lettering partially concealed, indicating French origin;[10] the lettering approximates as S F A T C S. Title information: "Serenata a Voce Sola con V.V. del Sgr. Alless.o | Scarlatti." Copyist: Sébastien de Brossard.

This serenata is no. XVI in a manuscript also containing sixteen cantatas and three arias by Scarlatti. A comparison of autograph manuscripts of works by Sébastien de Brossard confirms it is this avid collector's hand.[11] In addition, the library's catalogue contains the following annotations from Brossard himself:

All the contents are the most excellent modern [compositions], the composer's name alone is a convincing proof since he passed throughout all of Italy and even in all of Europe as the most accomplished musician who flourished at the end of last century and at the beginning of this one, of which we have already spent one quarter around this 4th May 1725; all the pieces I say are excellent, but amongst them, particularly *Piangea un di Fileno* no. IX; arias from the opera entitled *Emireno* no. X and following; the *Rossignol* no. XII; the cantatas entitled *Leandro* no. XIII [and] *Nerone* no. XIV; Serenata with solo voice and two violins and basso continuo no. XVI, et cetera.

Abbot Bousset, now the bishop of Troyes, brought them from Italy in the year 1699, and I copied them myself very carefully in the usual quarto, on white and unbound.[12]

This is the archetypal solo serenata. It has obbligato instrumental lines of two violins. It uses the first person direct address to the audience, in an outpouring of anguish over unrequited love. It is brimming with Petrarchan imagery such as water and burning flames symbolising ardent love, as well as a nocturnal opening with the Petrarchan *hor che* incipit discussed above in the "Historical Introduction" under "Common Features of Solo Serenatas." The vocal part ends with a long sustained fade, as the protagonist yearns for death.

At first glance, the serenata seems to have a strange structure: instrumental opening, recitative, five arias (the fourth with violins), concluding with a recitative and final aria. When one analyses the poetry, it can be seen that each of the five consecutive arias has one of only two rhyming patterns, *abba* or *abab*, with 3/8 used for the first and last aria in the series. It seems that the poet had in mind an aria with five strophes. Around the turn of the eighteenth century, the da capo aria replaced the more usual strophic structure.[13] This serenata may show a transitional stage: the setting of each strophe as if it were a new aria.

Prima d'esservi infedele (H. 578)

There are four extant sources:

A) Florence, Conservatorio Statale di Musica Luigi Cherubini (I-Fc), f-I.33 (previously D.2364), fols. 218r–233r. Watermark: fleur-de-lys in a double circle; also three mountains. No title information. Manuscript includes cantatas for soprano and violins (one including trumpet) by Alessandro Melani, and "Bella madre de' fiori" (not attributed). Copyist: other cantatas of Alessandro Scarlatti in the same hand are *Fileno, Idolo amato* and *Nacqui ai sospiri*.

B) Archivio dell'Abbazia di Montecassino (I-MC), 5-F-4b, fols. 17r–38r. Watermark: fleur-de-lys in a single circle. Title information: "Prima d'esservi infedele:- | Serenata a voce Sola | con V:V:- | Del Sig:re Alessandro | Scarlatti." In a collection of anonymous cantatas and some that identify Alessandro Scarlatti as the composer (including *Bella Donna di nome Santa*). Copyist: Naples, Scribe B (see *Eurilla, amata Eurilla*, source A).

C) Paris, Bibliothèque nationale de France (F-Pn), Vm⁷61ᵇⁱˢ, fols. 67v–73v. Watermarks alternate between a bunch of grapes and block lettering partially concealed, indicating French origin;[14] the lettering approximates as S F A T C S. Title information: "Clori fedele. ò Cantata del Sigʳ Alessandro Scarlatti | a voce Sola con 2 VV." Copyist: Sébastien de Brossard (see *Hor che l'aurato nume* above).

D) Cardiff Public Libraries, Central Library (GB-CDp), M.C.1.16 (viewed in facsimile only),[15] fols. 75r–91v. Title information: "Prima d'esservi | infedele:- | Serenata a voce Sola con V.V. | Del Sig:re Alessandro Scarlatti." Copyist: possibly an early sample of Tarquinio Lanciani.[16]

All sources are very reliable. Sources A and B are in the hands of regular scribes of serenatas, and source D, a hand seen often in association with Alessandro Scarlatti manuscripts. Source C is a French copy in the hand of Brossard, like *Hor che l'aurato nume*. Source A has more detail as regards basso continuo figures. A very interesting aspect of this serenata is that it returns to its initial poetic and musical idea at the end of the work. In sources A, B, and D this is written out in full. In source C, it is notated as a da capo of the beginning. A difference between the sources is whether the protagonist is speaking in the female or male voice. Sources A and C use feminine adjective endings ("-a," as in "sospira" in m. 17 of the recitative "Ma se con bella fede"), whereas sources B and D use the masculine ("-o"). It is interesting that the performance practice issue of gender of soloist required the amendment of the text, for at least one source.

Perché tacete, regolati concenti? (H. 551)

There are two extant sources:

A) Münster, Santini-Bibliothek (D-MÜs), Hs. 3910, fols. 1r–33v. Watermark: fleur-de-lys in a double circle. Title information: "Cantata Alto solo con VV. | Del Sig.ʳ Alessandro | Scarlatti." Copyist: Rome, Copyist XIII.[17]

B) Paris, Bibliothèque nationale de France (F-Pn), Rés. Vmc ms. 66, fols. 96r–140r with misnumbered pages. Watermark: bunches of grapes, indicating French origin;[18] block lettering. Title information: "Serenata | Con Violini | & | Basso." Copyist: unknown hand.

The Hanley catalogue does not list source B, but it does refer to a manuscript formerly held by the Institut de Musicologie de l'Université, Strasbourg, which the library reported as lost.[19]

As source A is in a hand that is frequently observed in manuscripts of Alessandro Scarlatti, it is clearly the primary source. Source B is a later, presumably eighteenth-century copy. It has many inconsistencies in spelling, accidentals, and even clef: this work for alto begins erroneously in soprano clef, and the notation, if not the clef, changes to alto clef at the recitative "Ma che dissi? Tacete!" The clef then catches up to the notational change at the next aria "Tra le fiamme del mio duolo." Although it is more often than not unreliable, source B proved useful in cases where occasional notes and measures were omitted in the primary source. This means that it was copied from another source and is of interest for this and for the following reasons.

The final aria of this lengthy work is seemingly unusually short—only one strophe in source A. The serenata has four arias in total, and the other three two-strophe arias are at least twice as long as this final number. But according to source B, the final aria also has a second strophe. Although it is possible that it is an addition by an enthusiastic amateur, for reasons of balance it is retained in this edition.

It is also of interest that this is a transposed copy: source A is in D with a minor third, and source B is in C with a minor third. This may account for some of the discrepancies of accidentals in source B, but these could also be attributed to the fact that notational practice regarding accidentals was changing, and this later scribe did not fully understand the older style. An interesting possibility is that the manuscript from which source B was copied may also have been in the key of C with the flattened third, a key favored by Alessandro Scarlatti when setting texts on a nocturnal subject, and one that was particularly associated with the genre of the *serenata a voce sola* (see "Musical Style and Performance" under "Tonal Structure"). The title "serenata" is given in source B only.

Sotto l'ombra d'un faggio (H. 678)

There are four extant sources:

> A) Archivio dell'Abbazia di Montecassino (I-MC), 5-F-4c, fols. 39r–46v. Watermark: fleur-de-lys in a single circle. Title information: "Sotto l'ombra d'un faggio:- | Serenata a voce Sola con VV:- | Del Sig.:re Alessandro | Scarlatti." In a collection of anonymous cantatas and some that identify Alessandro Scarlatti as the composer (including *Bella Donna di nome Santa*). Copyist: Naples, Scribe B (see *Eurilla, amata Eurilla*, source A).

> B) Conservatoire de Paris (F-Pc), X-638 (examined only as a reproduction). Title information: "Cantata con V.V. del Sigr. Alless.º Scarlatti." Copyist: unknown hand.

> C) Rome, Biblioteca Apostolica Vaticana (I-Rvat), Vat. lat. 10204. Title information: "Cantate per Musica | a voce sola | di Fran:co Maria | Paglia." Text only, identifying Francesco Maria Paglia as the author.

> D) London, Royal Academy of Music (GB-Lam), XXVI.C.272/79. Not consulted, incomplete.[20]

Source C, a text-only manuscript, contains seventy-two texts, many of which indicate a composer to whom the text is destined to be set. Of the collection, three are specifically titled as serenatas: *Ombre negre ed oscure* (Alessandro Melani is indicated); *La dove al sonno in braccio* (Alessandro Scarlatti is indicated, but the musical work has not survived, if it was indeed set); and *Taceva il mondo* (no composer indicated). *Sotto l'ombra d'un faggio* is number 69 in the collection and is not given the title "serenata."

The da capo arias "Sciglietemi, lasciatemi" and "Io dormivo presso un rivo" are written out in full in source A.

Notte, ch'in carro d'ombre (H. 480)

There is one extant source:

> Münster, Santini-Bibliothek (D-MÜs), Hs. 3937, fols. 1r–39v. Watermark: fleur-de-lys in a double circle. Title information (in copyist's hand): "Serenata | Soprano Solo con V.V. | Del Sigre Alessandro Scarlatti." The work occupies exactly ten bifolia, numbered by the copyist on the top inside of each bifolium. Copyist: Roman hand associated with Scarlatti (see below).

A table of contents, in a later hand and on a separate sheet, gives the following list: "Notte ch'in carro d'Ombre – Serenata a Cº con Violini"; "Al fragor di lieta tromba, Serenata a 3 con Ripieni e Stromenti"; "Il Giardino d'Amore – Serenata a C. e A. con Strom."

Details of the remaining works, as they appear in the scores themselves, are as follows:

> Title information: "Serenata à 3 Voci con Ripieni, e più Istrumenti | del Sigr. Alessandro Scarlatti | Al fragor di lieta tromba."

> Title information: "Il Giardino d'Amore | Serenata à 2: C. A. | con violini, Flautino è Tromba | Venere e Adone | del Sigr. Alesso. Scarlatti | Care selve, amati orrori."

The copyist of *Notte, ch'in carro d'ombre* appears to be from the circle of Alessandro Scarlatti on the evidence of MÜs 3903. The beautifully formed stave brace is one of the characteristics of this hand. At least one of the works copied by him in MÜs 3903, *Quale al gelo s'adugge*, is likely to have been copied from the autograph "Cantata Diary" (1704/5), described by Reinhard Strohm in his study, "Scarlattiana at Yale."[21] Scarlatti's oratorio *Il Giardino di Rose* (1707, MÜs 3861) is one of the major works in which this copyist also played a part. This hand appears again in GB-Lbl 14165.

The text of this cantata is one that seems to have held special interest for Scarlatti. His continuo cantata *Notte cara*, copied twice by the same copyist (in MÜs 3903 and Lbl 14165), shares some of its text, as well as the copyist, with the serenata *Notte, ch'in carro d'ombre*, notably the recitative "E tu, ch'ognor ti vanti" and the aria "Veloce e labile." The serenata text is in turn based on that of Antonio Cesti's cantata *Quanto sete per me pigri, o momenti*, with a number of consecutive lines quoted verbatim from the poem by Apolloni.[22] The principal part of the text shared with the original Apolloni poem is in the recitative and aria named above, and in the recitative "Ma parmi ch'esaudite," lines 1–4. Hanley considered *Notte cara* (H. 478, dated 1705 in MÜs 3903) to be "partly a renovation of that of No. 480" [*Notte, ch'in carro d'ombre*]; however the derivation of the text in the work of ca. 1660 was probably unknown to Hanley.[23] Since there is more in common between the Apolloni original and *Notte, ch'in carro d'ombre*, we may assume that the serenata pre-dates the cantata *Notte cara*, which retains just the final four lines of the recitative "E tu, ch'ognor ti vanti," culminating in the first line used by Cesti for his refrain, "Quanto s[i]ete per me pigri momenti." The continuo cantata *Notte cara* contains an aria with virtuoso cello writing on the text "Veloce e labile" (cf. "Rapido e labile," Apolloni/Cesti).

The da capo of each aria is written out in full, as is common in Roman manuscript sources, and has been checked in case of dubious readings, but in most cases the da capo version matches the first section in detail. *Fine* measures are adopted and reported from these da capo versions. All recitative and aria designations, other than that of the recitative "Ma parmi ch'esaudite," are editorial: the source gives tempo markings only.

Hor che di Febo ascosi (H. 511)

There are two extant sources and one source that is known to be lost:

> A) Münster, Santini-Bibliothek (D-MÜs), Hs. 3936. Watermark: fleur-de-lys in a double circle. Title information: "Serenata Soprano solo con V.V. | Hor che di Febo ascosi | Del Sigr: Alessº: Scarlatti." The manuscript contains only the single work; the twenty-five folios are not numbered. Copyist: the hand may be identifiable with copyist VIII in Watanabe's identification scheme,[24] one of the Roman copyists most commonly seen in manuscripts of Alessandro

Scarlatti's music, and particularly in the first decade of the eighteenth century.

B) Naples, Conservatorio di Musica San Pietro a Majella (I-Nc), Ms. 34.5.10, fols. 29r–40r. Watermark: animal in a single circle. Title information: "Raccolta di Cantate | del Cavalier | D'Alesso. Scarlatti." This heading is apparently in two or even three hands and was probably written at different times; the use of the title "Cavalier" suggests a copy date post 1716—however, it is clearly a later addition; the composer's name is given in the hand of the copyist.

C) No longer extant: Hanley cites Darmstadt, Hessische Landes- und Hochschulbibliothek (D-DS), Sammelband Mus. 5910. "Library reports that this copy was burned in wartime bombing. Strüver reports that it bore the date 1704."[25]

As is often the case in Roman manuscripts, the da capo arias in source A are written out in full, though only the first two of the four arias are da capo. Dynamic markings are unusually plentiful in the aria "Vago fior, ch'in notte algente."

In source B, the table of contents gives the titles of twenty-eight cantatas or single arias, of many types and periods, ranging from works of the 1690s (*A voi che l'accendeste*) to late works such as *Là dove a Mergellina* (1725). Mainly works for a solo voice and basso continuo, several works "con V.V." or "con Orch." are also included. Giuseppe Scarlatti is named towards the end of this wide-ranging anthology, but the majority of the works are certainly by Alessandro Scarlatti and represent what may have been regarded as a collection of highlights drawn from the composer's output for solo voice. A wide range of scribal hands and watermarks (mainly the animal in circle and fleur-de-lys in double circle) appears in this manuscript collection.

Source B presents a good clear copy of the work, closely related to source A in almost all details, though lacking the dynamic markings of the Rome source. At times the figuring is more complete or more accurate. The designation "Serenata" does not appear. The "Da Capo" marking is used, with A sections written out only once (unlike the Roman copy). Some minor differences in the poetic and musical text are reported below.

Source A has been treated as the primary source, with source B used as a reliable second source. Some readings from source B, possibly made with access to the (missing) autograph, have been adopted in the edition where source A seems clearly in error (source B is not based on source A).

Editorial Methods

Title information for the serenatas includes reference to the voice and any instruments, so that in the edition, part names have not been added to the scores. Abbreviations in these titles and in source instructions, tempi, etc., are tacitly written out. The placement of tempo indications is regularized in the edition to appear at the top of a system. Clefs have been normalized to those in modern use, so that vocal parts in the soprano or alto clefs have been transposed to the treble G clef. Key signatures have been retained in the form of the original sources. Time signatures are shown unchanged, except that the triple meters ($\frac{3}{8}$, $\frac{3}{4}$, $\frac{3}{2}$) are commonly expressed with a ₵ prefix by Scarlatti, a feature preserved in many contemporary copies, but not in this edition. Scarlatti's habit of barring arias in triple meter in units of two measures is also retained by a number of copyists; equally, it is disregarded by some copyists close to the composer. Irregular barring has been standardized but is reported in the critical notes.

Most editorial additions to the scores, such as added performance instructions, figures in the basso continuo, and so on, are enclosed in square brackets. Slurs and ties that are added are dashed. Editorial letter dynamics are set in bold type rather than the customary bold-italic.

Accidentals in square brackets indicate accidentals missing in the original source(s). Those in parentheses indicate editorial suggestions; these arise either where two readings are possible or where retention of the original key signature makes a cautionary accidental useful. In the period covered by the repertoire of this volume—the late seventeenth and early eighteenth centuries—both composer and copyists frequently used accidentals for an emphatic and/or cautionary function, many of which are regarded as unnecessary in modern usage. A typical example would be the interval of an augmented fourth (occurring in a melodic or bass line), such as B-flat to E; the seventeenth-century practice is to indicate both B-flat and E-natural, often regardless of the key signature, as if to underline and confirm the interval. These accidentals have been retained, as they serve a function to the performer that is more than mere outdated redundancy. Accidentals of the source that are preceded by an editorially added accidental for the same pitch within the same measure have also been retained, while those rendered redundant by a previous source accidental have been tacitly removed.

Basso continuo figures are a compilation of the sources. In some manuscripts, such as the source of *Sventurati miei penzieri*, basso continuo figures are expressed principally in the form of a flat or a sharp notated on the bass stave to indicate whether a chord is to have a major or minor third. The three-symbol system of sharp, flat, and natural (in which the natural expresses a minor third in a sharp key, for example) was not consistently adopted until the later part of Scarlatti's career, but it is in evidence already in *All'hor che stanco il sole*. Thus Scarlatti's works are transitional in this respect. The edition adopts the three-symbol system throughout; this applies not only to the bass figures but to accidentals notated in the vocal and instrumental lines as well.

The edition retains the figured bass convention of Scarlatti and his copyists in giving the cadential 4-3 without indicating the raised leading note as ♯3. It was the practice of Scarlatti to give the cadential 4-3 in one stroke of the pen. However, he regularly marks the third with a flat or a natural, if the expected leading note is to be contradicted.

An issue of rhythmic notation that arises in some arias is that Scarlatti commonly notates the same figure using dotted notes for instrumental parts, but without dotted notes for the vocal part, for example in the aria "Con l'idea d'un bel gioire" in *Notte, ch'in carro d'ombre,* or the aria "Se la sorte avesse in seno" in *Prima d'esservi infedele.* This is a regular feature of Scarlatti's notational practice that has been retained, though it is not suggested that it indicates a different approach between vocal and instrumental performance. Rather, it seems that singers would be routinely expected to adopt long/short patterns without prompting other than that of the text, whereas instrumentalists would require the prompting of notated dotted rhythms to initiate long/short patterns (suggesting that singers regularly altered notated rhythms in accordance with the text).[26]

Related to rhythmic articulation is the representation of beaming practices in seventeenth- and eighteenth-century manuscripts. In notation of vocal parts, beaming is of utmost importance as the primary means of indicating underlay of the text, and to this end, the sources almost always use beams for melismas and separately flagged notes for single words and syllables. This practice is tacitly regularized in the edition. In instrumental parts there usually appear to be no consistent principles at work, either in Scarlatti's autograph scores or in the work of copyists close to him; thus, beaming of instrumental parts follows the most commonly adopted patterns in the principal source.

Showing the *Fine* measure of da capo arias is an issue that arises in the eighteenth-century works. It was common for Roman copyists of the period covered by these works to write out da capo sections in full, and thus to notate the final measure of the aria precisely, perhaps using their own initiative as to the duration of the final note and rests to complete the measure. If necessary for clarity, *Fine* measures in the edition are shown as part of a first-time/second-time measure (as in *Notte, ch'in carro d'ombre,* the arias "Vieni, o Notte," "Veloce e labile," and "Con l'idea d'un bel gioire"). In several of these works, a new variant on the opening ritornello links the B section to the return of the A; these are indicated with dal segno markings, which indeed appear in the anonymous serenata *Era l'oscura notte* (as a cross sign with either two or four dots). Following from the repetition of material in fully notated da capo sections, corrections to the music that appear in the repeated section are adopted tacitly.

Dynamic markings, normally displayed as *pia.* and *for.* or *p* and *f*, are not always aligned with phrasing, for example, in *Notte, ch'in carro d'ombre,* where changes of dynamic level sometimes appear to be written before a rest or a phrase repetition. In such cases, they are repositioned. Dynamics in the edition are regularized to the modern symbols *p* and *f*. Trill indications, marked by *x* in some sources, have likewise been set using the modern symbol *tr*. Where the source has fermatas in some parts but not others, those missing are added tacitly.

Tutti and *solo* markings appear in the aria "Con l'idea d'un bel gioire" of *Notte, ch'in carro d'ombre,* but their exact significance is not clear. The *solo* markings appear in violin 1 (mm. 23 and 58—the latter moved to the last note of m. 57 in the edition) but are not answered by any *tutti* marking in that part; instead, there is a single *tutti* marking placed between the two violin parts (m. 70). Given the absence of *tutti* markings in violin 1, it is possible that its *solo* markings do not indicate a distinction between solo and tutti but instead simply emphasize that the violin 1 part is playing alone, without violin 2, and in dialogue with the voice. Tutti entries marked *piano* occur in similar passages by Scarlatti, for example in the autograph cantata *Su la sponda del mare (L'Olimpia),* H. 697 (Vienna, Österreichische Nationalbibliothek [A-Wn], SA.67.G.100). In this work, all *tutti* markings appear in violin 1 only and coincide with the reentry of all parts. There is thus the possibility in this type of chamber work that the *solo/tutti* markings are cautionary to violin 1, in an assumed ensemble of one to a part.

The texts of the serenatas are based on the music sources. As surviving autographs of other works show, it was the practice of Alessandro Scarlatti to punctuate the text in meticulous detail, particularly in recitatives, indicating the importance of punctuation to him in the compositional process. No attempt has been made in the edition to second-guess how his composed text in the lost autograph may have looked. For the edition, the text has been modernized, with capitalization regularized, and with punctuation—sparingly and inconsistently applied in the sources—added for sense.

Critical Notes

The following abbreviations are used in these critical notes: V = voice, Vn. = violin, B. = Basso, B.c. = Basso continuo (referring to figures). References to specific sources use the sigla noted in the source discussions above (I-Nc, F-Pn, etc.). Notes are numbered consecutively within a measure; where appropriate, beats are counted rather than notes. Pitches are identified using the system in which c' = middle C.

Sventurati miei penzieri

[Arioso e Recitativo]—[Aria]

M. 2, V, note 5 is d".   M. 12, V, dotting has been added for conformity with surrounding measures.   M. 19, V, notes 3–4 are undotted (cf. m. 12); note 4 is d" (cf. mm. 10–12).   M. 20, V, notes 3–4 are undotted (cf. m. 13); note 3 is b♭' (cf. mm. 10–12).   M. 21, V, note 4 is b♭' (cf. mm. 10–12).   M. 37, B., note 2 is A.   M. 56, B., note 3 is G. M. 59, B., note 2 is B♭.   M. 63, B., note 2 is c.   M. 79, B., notes 2–4 read B♭–c–d.   M. 95 and following, the aria is marked ³⁄₂ but is barred mostly in ⁶⁄₂; in the edition, the barring has been standardized to ³⁄₂.   M. 140, V, note 3 is b♭' (cf. m. 97).   M. 143, B., note 3 is half note (cf. m. 100). M. 168, B., note 2 is G (cf. mm. 105, 125, 148).

Eurilla, amata Eurilla

The continuo figures are a compilation of sources I-Nc, F-Pn, and B-Bc.

1. [Recitativo]

Mm. 1–4, see discussion under "Sources" regarding the variant form of the incipit.

2. [Aria]

Mm. 6 and 7, text of I-Nc gives "non ho" in place of "più cor" (cf. F-Pn, B-Bc, GB-Lcm).   M. 11, B., note 6, I-Nc gives e. (cf. F-Pn, B-Bc, GB-Lcm).   M. 13, B., notes 1–3, I-Nc gives two 16th notes followed by 8th (cf. F-Pn and GB-Lcm).   M. 23, B., note 1, I-Nc is dotted quarter note with no 8th rest; reading follows B-Bc and GB-Lcm. M. 24, B., note 5, I-Nc and F-Pn give f♯ with B.c. figure ♯ (cf. m. 1, B., and m. 4, V, as well as B-Bc).

3. Recitativo

M. 6, B., note 1, the editorial (♯) is one solution to this problematic bar; another would be to leave out this suggestion, but add ♯ to V, notes 5 and 6.

4. [Aria]

In I-Nc both strophes are written under the same music, whereas in F-Pn, B-Bc, and GB-Lbl both strophes are written out in full. The time signature of this aria is given as 3/8 in all versions, but the barring changes between 6/8 and 3/8 meter, except in B-Bc, which is barred entirely according to 3/8; in the edition, the barring has been standardized to 3/8.

All'hor che stanco il sole

1. [Sinfonia]

Upbeat to m. 13, repeat bar added editorially.   M. 19, Vn. 1, note 5 is c″.   M. 27, repeat bar added editorially.

2. [Recitativo]

M. 25, Vn. 1, note 10 is c″.   M. 27, Vn. 2, beat 2, dotted 8th and 16th note (cf. Vn. 1 and m. 26, beat 4).   M. 27, Vn. 2, notes 7–13 are a′–b♭′–a′–b♭′–c″–b♭′–a′.   M. 30, Vn. 2, note 10 is f′.   M. 32, Vn. 2, notes 7–10 are g′–a′–g′–a′.

3. [Aria]

M. 16, B., note 7 is c.   M. 27, Vn. 2, notes 5–6 are g′–f′ (cf. m. 11).

4. [Aria]

This aria is marked 3/2 but is barred in 6/2; in the edition, the barring has been standardized to 3/2.   M. 19, B., note 6 is c.   M. 37, Vn. 2, note 1 is e″.

6. [Aria]

This aria is marked 3/4 but is barred in 6/4; in the edition, the barring has been standardized to 3/4.   M. 6, B., note 1 is g.   M. 12, V, note 1 is d″ (cf. m. 18, Vn. 1).   M. 20, Vn. 1, note 2 is c″ (cf. m. 14, V).   M. 21, Vn. 2, note 2 is b♭′ (cf. m. 33).   M. 41, Vn. 2, note 2 is b♭′ (cf. m. 33).

7. [Recitativo]

M. 3 is marked 3/4 but the following measures are barred in 6/4; in the edition, the barring has been standardized to 3/4.

8. [Aria]

M. 6, Vn. 2, notes 3–5 are e″–e″–c″.   M. 9, Vn. 2, notes 2–3 are b♭′–c″.   M. 30, V, note 5 is e′ (cf. m. 8, Vn. 1).

10. [Aria]

M. 8, Vn. 2, note 1 is g′ (cf. m. 5, V).

12. [Recitativo]—[Aria]

M. 3, Vn. 2, note 3 is g′.   M. 7, B., note 1 is f.   M. 16, V, notes 1–2 are undotted (cf. m. 2, Vn. 1, and m. 31, V).

13. [Recitativo]

M. 22, Vn. 2, note 5 is e′.

Hor che l'aurato nume

1. Sonata

M. 10, B.c., note 4, figure is ♭.   M. 12, repeat bar added editorially.   M. 26, Vn. 2, note 8 has trill indicated.

2. [Recitativo]

M. 13, B.c., beat 2, the slur, in addition to a *legato* marking, may indicate that the figure is to be held over.

3. Aria

M. 5 and similar bars, B.c., see m. 13 of recitativo above. Mm. 40–41 and 45–46, an alternative reading for these measures is with the addition of editorial B-naturals, confirming the previous key of C minor.   M. 45, V, notes 1–2 are undotted (cf. m. 40).   M. 65, V, notes 1–2 are undotted (cf. m. 40).

5. Aria

This aria is marked 3/4 but is barred mostly in 6/4; in the edition, the barring has been standardized to 3/4.   M. 21, V, syllable "-na" on note 2; moved to m. 22 in edition.

6. [Aria]

M. 3, B., notes 3–4 are undotted (cf. mm. 8, 9, 22, 23). M. 5, Vn. 2, note 8 is b♭′.   M. 6, Vn. 2, note 5 has trill indicated.

7. [Aria]

This aria is marked 3/8 but is barred mostly in 6/8; in the edition, the barring has been standardized to 3/8.   M. 7, B., notes 1–2 are undotted (cf. mm. 16, 34, 82).   M. 69, V, note 3 is f″ (cf. mm. 12, 21).

9. [Aria]

M. 12, Vn. 2, note 3 is g′.

Prima d'esservi infedele

1. [Introdutione]

M. 5, B.c., note 4, figure is ♭.   M. 14, I-Fc has double bar after beat 1.   M. 35 (at the *Largo assai*) is marked 3/2 but the following measures are barred in 6/2 in I-Fc; in the edition, the barring has been standardized to 3/2.   Mm. 36–45, V, slurs not indicated in I-Fc.   M. 44, B.c., figure 6/5 is given on beat 1 in I-MC and on beat 2 in I-Fc.

2. Recitativo

M. 12, beat 1, I-MC gives half note and therefore the barring is different to the end of this recitative.   Mm.

27–28, V, text is "saprei" in I-MC. M. 30, B., note 4 is e♭ in I-MC. M. 31, B., beat 1 is g–G 8th notes in I-MC.

3. Aria

Mm. 7 and 11, V, dynamics appear in I-MC only. M. 13, B., note 5 is d in I-Fc. Mm. 18–19, V, text in second strophe is "piange" in I-Fc. M. 42, B., note 1 is d in I-Fc. M. 43, a single measure is given to the F-major chord, and the ritornello begins on a new measure by reiterating it (in I-Fc, I-MC, and GB-CDp); the F-Pn source gives the overlap of the final bar of the aria and ritornello, and this is retained in order to reflect a common performance practice. M. 48, Vn. 2, beat 2 is f″–f′–g′–a′ (all 16th notes) in I-Fc, and f′–g′–a′ (two 16ths and one 8th) in I-MC; edition follows reading in GB-CDp. M. 50, Vn. 2, beat 3 is e″–e″ (8ths) in I-Fc; this measure is missing in GB-CDp. M. 52, B., note 1 is f in I-MC and GB-CDp. M. 53, repeat bar added editorially.

4. [Recitativo]

M. 6, V, notes 1–3 slurred in I-MC. M. 8, no double bar or "Segue" in I-Fc. Mm. 16–17, B., no tie in I-Fc.

5. Aria

M. 11, B., note 8 is D in I-Fc. M. 12, B., note 6 is D in I-Fc. M. 14, B., notes 8–9 are undotted (cf. m. 15). M. 21, B.c., note 2, figure is ♭. M. 25 and following, all parts, triplets are notated in groups of three 16th notes, as is customary with Scarlatti's notational practice.

Perché tacete, regolati concenti?

1. Sinfonia

M. 1, B., note 4, ♯ given in F-Pn only. M. 4, Vn. 2, note 5 has ♯ in F-Pn; if it is adopted then note 4 must also be sharpened. M. 6, Vn. 1, note 4, ♯ given in F-Pn only. M. 27, repeat bar added editorially. M. 32, Vn. 2, note 4 is g′. M. 55, Vn. 1, note 2 is g′. M. 57, B., note 2 is a. M. 69, Vn. 2, note 1 is d″ in D-MÜs (cf. F-Pn). M. 81, B., note 4 is e (cf. m. 82, B., note 5). M. 83, repeat bar added editorially.

3. Aria

M. 26, B., note 6 lacks ♭ in D-MÜs (cf. F-Pn). M. 29, Vn. 2, note 8 lacks ♭ in D-MÜs (cf. F-Pn). M. 31, repeat bar added editorially.

5. [Aria]

This aria is marked 3/8 but is frequently barred in 6/8; in the edition, the barring has been standardized to 3/8. M. 4, B., note 3 has no ♭ in both manuscripts and in every recurrence (mm. 15, 22, 71). M. 12, repeat bar added editorially. M. 66, Vn. 1, note 3 is d″ in both sources. M. 89, Vn. 2, notes 3–4 have dotted rhythm in second strophe and in both strophes of F-Pn. M. 90, repeat bar added editorially.

6. [Recitativo]

M. 17, V, note 7 is f′ (cf. m. 16, V, note 3).

7. [Aria]

This aria is marked 3/4 but is frequently barred in 6/4; in the edition, the barring has been standardized to 3/4. M. 12, B., note 1 is missing in D-MÜs (cf. F-Pn). M. 23, B., note 3 is missing in D-MÜs (cf. F-Pn). Mm. 32–36, B., these bars are empty in D-MÜs; edition follows F-Pn. M. 67, B., note 5 has ♭ (cf. m. 69). M. 86, repeat bar added editorially.

9. [Aria]

In this aria, the second strophe appears in F-Pn only, which is written out in full. In the F-Pn second strophe, "con destare" appears in mm. 7–8 and "al destare" in mm. 9–10; "col destare" is adopted for meaning and style. Mm. 14–15, D-MÜs uses the text of the F-Pn second strophe, rather than a repeat of the text at mm. 11–13.

Sotto l'ombra d'un faggio

1. [Introdutione]

M. 14, Vn. 1, notes 3–4 are undotted in I-MC (cf. m. 2 and F-Pc). M. 20, B., note is E in F-Pc. Mm. 24–25, text, I-Rvat gives "Partenio" (not "Fileno") as the protagonist. M. 38, B.c., note 5 has figure ♯ in F-Pc.

2. Aria

The da capo is written out in I-MC, giving a fermata on beat 4 of the final bar. M. 26, Vn. 2, notes 7–9 are 8th–16th–16th notes in I-MC (cf. F-Pc).

3. Recitativo

Mm. 12–13, text, I-Rvat gives "Lesba la ninfa" in place of "Filli la vaga." M. 14, V, notes 6, 7, and 8 are d″ in I-MC (cf. F-Pc).

4. Aria

This aria is marked 3/8 but is frequently barred in 6/8; in the edition, the barring has been standardized to 3/8. M. 11 and subsequently, the original beaming implies a hemiola. M. 58, B., note 5 is 8th note g in I-MC (cf. m. 61 and F-Pc). M. 66, Vn. 1, note 3 is f″ in I-MC (cf. F-Pc).

6. Aria

M. 4, Vn. 1, note 2 lacks ♯ in I-MC. M. 7, V, note 7 is b′ in I-MC (cf. F-Pc).

Notte, ch'in carro d'ombre

1. [Introdutione]

M. 5, B., note 6 is c♯. M. 34, Vn. 1, notes 2–4 are e″–c♯″–f♯″, producing fifths with Vn. 2 and clearly incorrect with B.; transposition down a third is the suggested reading. M. 35, Vn. 1, notes 1–2 are b′–g′.

3. [Aria]

M. 20, Vn. 2, note 7 is tied to next measure.

5. [Aria]

M. 12, B., rhythm in da capo is two half notes (no quarter rest). M. 26, B., note 1 is c. M. 41, *Fine* measure on da capo, V and B. have whole notes, Vn. has half note and half rest; set as second-time measure in edition.

7. [Aria]

Both tempo markings appear in source, *adagio* over Vn. 1, *Largo* below Vn. 2 and B. staves.   M. 17, B., note 1 appears to be a♭, but b♭ is adopted in edition since the resulting IV–V–I progression parallels the cadential progression in mm. 53 and 64; this also applies to m. 21, an octave lower.   M. 18, Vn. 1, placement of dynamic *p* is under note 1, but more likely applies to note 2.   Mm. 23, 24, 25, 28, 29, 30, 42, 49, 58, 59, 60, 61, 63, 64, 66, 67, 68, 69, V, notated rhythm of notes 1–2 is two 16ths, while Vn. 1 has dotted 16th note plus 32nd note figure in the same measures, but note that V is dotted on this figure in mm. 71 and 72; similarly, see mm. 39, 40, 46, 47, V, notes 3–4, m. 65, notes 2–3, and m. 74, notes 1–2, where notes are 16ths against dotted rhythm in the instruments; the source notation in all these measures has been retained, but performers are alerted that the different notation almost certainly does not indicate intended rhythmic differentation in performance; dotted performance is in most cases the preferable option (see the editorial methods). M. 47, Vn. 1, notes 3–4 are even 16ths in da capo.   M. 50, Vn. 1, notes 3–4 are even 16ths; dotted rhythm adopted in edition as seen in B. (also da capo) and Vn. 2 (first section). M. 58, Vn. 1, note 1 has *solo;* moved to m. 57 in edition.

8. [Recitativo]

M. 4, V, notes 1–2, text is "Oimè."

9. [Aria]

M. 27, *Fine* measure on da capo, Vn., V, B. have quarter note, quarter rest, half rest.   M. 34, Vn., note 2 is a′; g′ chosen to continue the descending line.   Mm. 36 and 44, V has "fine al mio" with "mar-" slurred on notes 1–2 of following measure; in the edition, underlay without elision on "fi-ne al" brings "mio mar-tir" to mm. 37 and 45. *Fine* for serenata indicated after final barline, between Vn. and V staves.

Hor che di Febo ascosi

1. Introdutione

I-Nc has *Sinf.ᵃ*; edition follows D-MÜs with *Introdutione*.   M. 7, I-Nc has *adagio* above B. stave; edition follows D-MÜs with *and:ᵉ* below B. stave.   M. 15, Vn. 1, "f" written over note 2 in D-MÜs.   Mm. 21–23, dynamic markings in D-MÜs only.

2. Recitativo

I-Nc has *attacca sub.[it]o* on blank stave above this recitative, which is set as the continuation of the introduzione.   Punctuation for text underlay found only in D-MÜs.   M. 2, B.c., beat 3 has figure 2 in I-Nc only.   M. 3, V, notes 4–5, underlay is "d'An-fi-" (two separately flagged notes) in I-Nc so that "-tri-te" falls on notes 6 and 7 as quarter notes; edition follows D-MÜs.   Mm. 9–10, V, text is "d'un Amante" in I-Nc; edition follows D-MÜs. M. 12, V, notes 7–8, text is "cor" (quarter note tied to 8th) in D-MÜs; edition follows I-Nc.   M. 15, V, trill marking in I-Nc only.

3. Aria

I-Nc has *Grave* below B. stave; edition follows D-MÜs with *Grave e pia.* to the left of Vn. 1 and Vn. 2 staves.   M. 1, I-Nc has *ad:[agio]* below Vn. 1 stave.   M. 2, Vn. 1, D-MÜs lacks trill marking, but it is in da capo.   M. 7, V, I-Nc lacks trill marking, but it is in D-MÜs (though lacking in da capo).   M. 7, V, slur over notes 2–4 missing in D-MÜs, but slur over notes 2–3 is in da capo; edition follows reading in I-Nc.   M. 7, B., notes 5–6 missing in D-MÜs.   M. 10, V, "-pri" placed on note 6 in D-MÜs; edition follows I-Nc with "-pri" slurred on notes 5–6.   M. 10, B., note 4 is c♯ in D-MÜs (also da capo).   M. 17, B., note 7 is 16th note (following 8th and 16th rests) in D-MÜs (also da capo), but 8th note following 8th rest in identical mm. 14 and 18.   M. 22, *Fine* measure on da capo (in D-MÜs), quarter note all parts, no rests making up beats 2–4 of the measure.   Mm. 22 and 23, B.c., beat 4 has figure 5 in I-Nc only.   Mm. 24–27, 30–32, 32–35, V, text is "scuopri" in D-MÜs.   M. 35, I-Nc has fermatas on half rests with *Da capo* placed outside the double bar.

4. Recitativo

M. 1, V, note 6, text is "oh" (D-MÜs and I-Nc).   M. 5, V, note 2, text has semicolon in D-MÜs.   M. 12, *Siegue* in I-Nc.

5. Aria

The edition follows I-Nc for vocal slurs; D-MÜs only has slurs in mm. 4 (also da capo) and 19.   Mm. 19 and 25, V, notes 2–3, text is "bruggia" in I-Nc.   M. 30, *Da Capo subᵒ* in I-Nc.

6. Recitativo

M. 1, V, notes 1–2, text is "Pende" in D-MÜs; note 3, text is "da" in I-Nc.   M. 11, B.c., beat 3, figure is 4 in D-MÜs.   M. 12, B., note 4 is E in D-MÜs.   M. 17 is missing in D-MÜs; edition follows I-Nc.   M. 18, B., note 4 lacks ♭ in D-MÜs.   M. 23, *Siegue* in D-MÜs; *Siegue Aria con V.V.* in I-Nc.

7. Aria

This aria is marked ¢³⁄₈ in both sources and is barred in ⁶⁄₈ in I-Nc; in the edition, the barring has been standardized to ³⁄₈, as in D-MÜs.   Violin parts marked *solo* only in D-MÜs.   Dynamic markings only in D-MÜs.   M. 1, *à tempo lento* in D-MÜs; *andante Grave* in I-Nc.   M. 8, Vn. 1 and Vn. 2, note 1, *pia* in D-MÜs; editorial placement in m. 7 follows the phrasing.   Mm. 8, 11, and 12, Vn. 1 and Vn. 2, notes 2–4 are 16th notes in D-MÜs; edition follows I-Nc, and cf. m. 10, which gives two 32nds and one 8th in both sources.   M. 14, B., note 1 is c′ in I-Nc.   M. 16 missing in D-MÜs, and *for.* markings placed in m. 17 instead of 16.   M. 19, B., note 2 is g in D-MÜs.   Mm. 31 and 32 are combined in D-MÜs (i.e., vocal entry overlaps with the last note of the instrumental introduction, and the bass note is missing).   M. 68, V, notes 2–3 slurred in I-Nc, which places the syllable "-le" on the downbeat of m. 69, but separate beaming in m. 68 suggests *anticipazione;* the syllable is also placed in m. 69 in D-MÜs, but with no slur in m. 68 nor over the barline in mm. 68–69; cf. the parallel passages at mm. 86–87 and 90–91, where a slur over the barline clearly indicates that the syllable should be sung with the slur, though here too the syllable is written on the downbeat of mm. 87 and 91; the edition matches mm. 68–69 to the later passages, with an added dashed slur.   M. 88, V, notes 9–12 are d♭″–e♭″–d♭″–e♭″ in D-MÜs; the edition follows I-Nc.   M. 97, B.c., note 2 has figure $^6_4$ in D-MÜs.

9. Aria

This aria is marked $\mathbf{C}^3_4$ and is barred in $^6_4$ in I-Nc; in the edition, the meter is $^3_4$ and the barring is the same as in D-MÜs.   M. 16, B., note 2 is f♯ in D-MÜs; edition follows I-Nc and parallel passage in m. 23 of D-MÜs.   M. 34, Vn. 1, note 2 is g′ in both D-MÜs and I-Nc.   Mm. 42–43, 44–45, 48–49, V, text is "furor" in I-Nc; edition follows "splendor" in D-MÜs.   M. 44, Vn. 1, note 2 is g′ in D-MÜs.   M. 56, Vn. 2, note 5 is g″ in D-MÜs.   Mm. 57 and 58, V, text is "ad Dio" in D-MÜs.   M. 59, *Fine* for serenata in I-Nc.

Notes

1. Edwin Hanley, "Alessandro Scarlatti's 'Cantate da Camera': A Bibliographical Study" (Ph.D. diss., Yale University, 1963), 36.

2. See Dinko Fabris, "La serenata a Napoli prima di Alessandro Scarlatti," in *La serenata tra Seicento e Settecento: Musica, poesia, scenotecnica, Atti del convegno internazionale di studi, Reggio Calabria 16–17 maggio 2003*, ed. Nicolò Maccavino (Reggio Calabria: Laruffa Editore, 2007), 1:15–71.

3. See Hanley, "Alessandro Scarlatti's 'Cantate da Camera,' " 223.

4. Mauro Amato, "Le antologie di arie e di arie e cantate tardo-seicentesche alla Biblioteca del Conservatorio 'S. Pietro a Majella' di Napoli" (Ph.D. diss., Scuola di Paleografia e Filologia Musicale di Cremona, 1998), vol. 1, see especially pp. 42–44, p. 95 n. 50, and p. 96 n. 53.

5. Keiichiro Watanabe, "The Music-Paper Used by Handel and His Copyists in Italy, 1706–1710," in *Handel Collections and Their History*, ed. Terence Best (Oxford: Clarendon Press, 1993), 199.

6. Hanley, "Alessandro Scarlatti's 'Cantate da Camera,' " 223.

7. See *Eos: An Enquiry into the Theme of Lovers' Meetings and Partings at Dawn in Poetry*, ed. Arthur T. Hatto (The Hague: Mouton and Co., 1965). This book is a collection of essays, each focusing on poetry from a different culture. For the essay on Italian poetry of the early modern period, see R. Glynn Faithfull, "Italian," in particular pp. 393 and 408–9.

8. Aurelio Zonghi, *Zonghi's Watermarks* (Hilversum: Paper Publications Society, 1953), table 121, figures 1688–94.

9. Amato, "Le antologie di arie e di arie e cantate," 43.

10. William A. Churchill, *Watermarks in Paper in Holland, England, France, etc., in the XVII and XVIII Centuries and Their Interconnection* (Amsterdam: M. Hertzberger, 1935), 86, figures/watermarks cccli–cccliii.

11. See Sébastien de Brossard, *Cantates françaises et italiennes*, ed. Jérôme Dorival (Éditions du Centre de musique baroque de Versailles, 1997).

12. "Tout cela est du plus excellent moderne, le nom seul de l'auteur en est une preuve convaincante puisqu'il passe dans toute l'Italie et même dans toute l'Europe pour le musicien le plus accompli qui eut fleuri sur la fin du dernier siecle et au commencement de celuy y dont nous avons déja passé pres du quart au mois de may 1725; toutes ces pieces dis-je sont excellentes, mais entre autres et principalement celle qui commence par Piangea un di Fileno no. IX; arie dell'opera intitolato Emireno no. X et seqq.; le Rossignol no.XII; les cantates intitulées Leandro no. XIII; Nerone no. XIV, Serenata a C. solo cum 2 vv. et B. continuo no. XVI etca.

"Mr l'abbé Bossuet maintenant evêque de Troyes les aporta d'Italie l'an 1699, et je les copié moy même fort correctement dans un in 4o a l'ordinaire, en blanc et non relié."

13. Hanley, "Alessandro Scarlatti's 'Cantate da Camera,' " 70.

14. Churchill, *Watermarks in Paper*, 86, figures/watermarks cccli–cccliii.

15. Malcolm Boyd, ed., The Italian Cantata in the Seventeenth Century, vol. 13 (New York and London: Garland, 1986), 33–54.

16. Keiichiro Watanabe and Hans Joachim Marx, "Händels italienische Kopisten," in *Gedenkschrift für Jens Peter Larsen (1902–1988)*, ed. Hans Joachim Marx, vol. 3 of *Göttinger Händel-Beiträge* (Kassel: Bärenreiter, 1989), 198.

17. Watanabe and Marx, "Händels italienische Kopisten," 199.

18. Churchill, *Watermarks in Paper*, 86, figures/watermarks cccli–cccliii.

19. See Hanley, "Alessandro Scarlatti's 'Cantate da Camera,' " 391.

20. Hanley reports that the manuscript lacks violin parts and that the sinfonia and ritornelli are missing; see "Alessandro Scarlatti's 'Cantate da Camera,' " 464.

21. Reinhard Strohm, "Scarlattiana at Yale," in *Händel e gli Scarlatti a Roma, Atti del convegno internazionale di studi, Roma 1985*, ed. Nino Pirrotta and Agostino Ziino (Florence: Olschki, 1987), section 3, "Cantate da Camera by Alessandro Scarlatti," 122–39.

22. See Antonio Cesti, *Quanto sete per me pigri, o momenti!*, ed. Rosalind Halton, Web Library of Seventeenth-Century Music (http://aaswebsv.aas.duke.edu/wlscm), no. 8, 2007. Poem by Apolloni, "Ora aspettata da un Amante / Dell'Appolloni" [sic], Rome, Biblioteca Apostolica Vaticana (I-Rvat), Ferrajoli 1, fols. 233v–235v. The text is transcribed in the appendix of Paolo Mechelli, "Giovanni Filippo Apolloni: Riflessioni sui testi per le cantate di Cesti," in *La Figura e l'opera di Antonio Cesti*, ed. M. Dellaborra (Florence: Olschki, 2003), 263–64. My thanks to Barbara Sachs for drawing my attention to this source of the text, and for her work on preparing the text and translation for this edition of *Notte, ch'in carro d'ombre*.

23. Hanley, "Alessandro Scarlatti's 'Cantate da Camera,' " 348.

24. Keiichiro Watanabe, "Die Kopisten der Händel-Handschriften in der Santini-Bibliothek, Münster," *Ongakugaku [Journal of the Musicological Society of Japan]* 16 (1970): 244–45. In this important early study, Watanabe did not yet identify this hand with Domenico Castrucci, a subsequent claim (see Watanabe and Marx, "Händels italienische Kopisten," 228) that

has since been convincingly disproved by Ursula Kirkendale in "Handel with Ruspoli: New Documents from the Archivio Segreto Vaticano, December 1706 to December 1708," *Studi Musicali* 32 (2003): 316–17. The hand identified as "Copyist VIII" in Watanabe's 1970 article, however, matches that of MÜs 3936 in a number of important features.

25. Hanley, "Alessandro Scarlatti's 'Cantate da Camera,'" 369.

26. The issue is discussed in John Byrt, "Elements of Rhythmic Inequality in the Arias of Alessandro Scarlatti and Handel," *Early Music* 35 (2007): 609–26, and Rosalind Halton, "Correspondence: Rhythmic Inequality," *Early Music* 36 (2008): 350–51.

Appendix

Era l'oscura notte

The Authorship of *Era l'oscura notte*

Doubt has been cast on the authorship of *Era l'oscura notte: Serenata a voce sola con Strumenti* (H. 249) since Edwin Hanley noted (or rather implied) in his catalogue that the only basis for the attribution to Scarlatti is on the binding of the source, D-MÜs Hs. 3938: "Al.º Scarlatti named on binding."[1] But the attribution is not supported elsewhere in the manuscript, which contains only the single work. The copyist, who has been speculatively identified as Carl'Antonio Ferri (copyist XIII in Watanabe's scheme),[2] gives no attribution on the heading of the work, a rarity for this copyist with Scarlatti's works. Neither does the title page carry an attribution. Assuming that this was a copyist familiar with the composer's style and hand—one of Scarlatti's principal copyists in the late seventeenth century—we may conclude that there is no reason in the source, other than the binding mentioned by Hanley, for identifying Scarlatti as the composer.

Indeed, we may ask why an attribution to Scarlatti has been entertained at all. The simplest explanation is that the manuscript appears in a catalogued sequence of serenata and cantata manuscripts composed by Scarlatti. *Era l'oscura notte* is the odd one out with its lack of attribution to Scarlatti on the manuscript itself. But it does maintain a sequence of works designated as "Serenata Soprano Solo con Violini": the previous manuscripts in the sequence (D-MÜs 3936 and 3937) contain two Scarlatti works with comparable title pages and designations. Supposing that the manuscripts were transferred in this order to the Santini Collection, we may guess that the library from which it came had the works already grouped together.[3]

Though the music could hardly be regarded as characteristic of Scarlatti's style, this is not to be taken as a criticism of the work, simply recognition of its stylistic character. In her study of Scarlatti's cantatas with instruments, Cecilia Van de Kamp Freund considers the character of *Era l'oscura notte*, pointing out that "the ritornello themes are extremely bright and tuneful and rhythmically distinctive." She lists a number of "stylistic peculiarities" that would argue against accepting this as a work of Scarlatti. These include the elimination of the ritornello before the da capo; key relationships—the fact that all arias are in major keys; arias that are similarly constructed, with literal repetition of thematic material; the harmonic style, especially the absence of diminished sevenths and dissonances; and finally the absence of "voice-weaving techniques."[4]

To these points we may add several others. The second violin is mostly a filler part. It is uncharacteristic of Scarlatti to compose consecutive arias in $\frac{12}{8}$ meter (see the second and third arias). Ranges are unusual for Scarlatti, the vocal range of d to b♭" as well as the violin solo to f'". And the B section of the first aria ("Lo vedrai s'io son fedele o crudele") in itself presents some features that point away from Scarlatti. First, there is the alternation of tempo contrasts, Presto followed by Largo; marked tempo contrasts *between* A and B sections are certainly common in Scarlatti's writing, but *within* a single section is less characteristic. Second, the cadenza-like dialogue between violin solo and voice that completes the B section is unusual for Scarlatti.

The point made by Van de Kamp Freund about the omission of the ritornello music before the da capo is more contentious. But it would be difficult to point to a Scarlatti work in which "Dal Segno" is used so consistently with each aria. The double cross with dots on either side is not a sign associated with Scarlatti, who is more likely to indicate any omission of ritornello music by a music cue.

Considering the character and pacing of the music, we may speculate whether the anonymous composer of *Era l'oscura notte* may have intended to capture the style of Giovanni Bononcini, rather than that of Scarlatti. Bononcini's most popular work, the opera *Il trionfo di Camilla,* first performed in December 1696, has a striking number of arias in $\frac{12}{8}$, and the violin writing is not only inviting to the player—in a way that Scarlatti's rarely is—but shows the feature of regularly ranging over three strings, particularly at phrase ends, in the same way that we find in the second aria of this serenata. Arias are also found in *Camilla* that indulge in the trick of juxtaposing phrases in contrasted tempi (for example, the act 1 duet between Tullia and Linco, "Languisco, sospiro"). The easy-paced, open style that made the opera an immediate hit is also the predominant flavor of *Era l'oscura notte*—which is altogether a less intense composition than any of the solo serenatas attributed to Scarlatti.

It is of course impossible to prove or disprove an attribution on stylistic grounds alone: for every one of the above stylistic points, other than the absence of polyphonic writing, one might argue that examples exist in authenticated works of Scarlatti. It seems from the cataloguing of the work within a large group of works by Scarlatti that *Era l'oscura notte* was accepted in its period as a work of comparable status and function to the Scarlatti serenatas. With its overall structure of four recitatives and four arias, including the introductory accompanied recitative, it certainly fits the pattern of the other Scarlatti solo serenatas in the manuscript sequence. Bononcini, as the principal composer of equivalent reputation to Scarlatti at the turn of the century, seems a plausible alternative, but as Lowell Lindgren remarks, this setting may have been produced by any of the numerous cantata composers active in Rome at this time.[5] The work merits performance on its own terms, an attractive aside to the main dish of Scarlatti offered in this volume.

Notes

1. Edwin Hanley, "Alessandro Scarlatti's 'Cantate da Camera': A Bibliographical Study" (Ph.D. diss., Yale University, 1963), 221.

2. Keiichiro Watanabe and Hans Joachim Marx, "Händels italienische Kopisten," *Göttinger Händel-Beiträge* 3 (1989): 199. Ferri was described in the Giustificazioni of Casa Pamphili as "Copista del S.r Scarlatti." His hand is represented in this volume with the serenata *Perché tacete, regolati concenti?*, see plate 4.

3. Wladimir Stassoff, *L'Abbé Santini et sa collection musicale à Rome* (Florence, 1854), specifically mentions a group of manuscripts close to D-MÜs 3938 in his entry on Alessandro Scarlatti (p. 61), beginning the entry with the description "Un très grand nombre de cantates de chambre et d'airs de théâtres . . ." He then names works "Orphée, Endymion, Fenice, la partenza, cantates [sic]; cantate pastorale") that have the catalogue numbers 3931 ("L'Orfeo"), 3927 ("Endimione e Cintia"), 3928 ("La Fenice"), 3932 ("La Partenza"), and (assumed) 3926 (cantata "Notte di Natale," 1705). As the earliest publication on the Santini Collection, it may be assumed that this list represents a sample of manuscripts, mainly by Scarlatti, that were acquired and already kept together.

4. Cecilia Kathryn Van de Kamp Freund, "Alessandro Scarlatti's Duet Cantatas and Solo Cantatas with Obbligato Instruments" (Ph.D. diss., Northwestern University, 1979), 389–90.

5. I am most grateful to Lowell Lindgren for giving his opinion in a private communication on the authorship of *Era l'oscura notte*, which he agrees is unlikely to be a work of Scarlatti.

Text and Translation

Era l'oscura notte

1. [Recitativo]

Era l'oscura notte e d'ogni intorno
di fosco ammanto il ciel si ricopria
quasi che far volesse
con quei bruni apparati
una pompa funebre al morto giorno,
quando un misero amante,
per far palese la costante fede
dell'amoroso core
all'incredula Filli
che fido no 'l credea,
lagrimando,
sospirando,
tra lagrime e sospir così dicea.

It was dark night and all around
the sky was covered by a murky veil
as if it wanted to use
those mourning colors
for a funeral for the day that has died,
when an unhappy lover,
to make known the constancy
of his loving heart
to the incredulous Filli
who did not believe him faithful,
weeping,
sighing,
through his tears and sighs spoke thus.

2. Aria

"Lo vedrai s'io son fedele
o crudele
quando l'alma innamorata
dal mio petto fuggirà.
Perché sempre a te d'intorno
notte e giorno,
da' miei spirti agitata,
ombra ancor s'aggirerà.

"You will see if I am faithful
or cruel
when my loving soul
flees from my breast.
Because always around you
night and day,
agitated by my spirits,
my shade will stay by you.

3. Recitativo

"E dove, amato bene,
tu volgerai le piante,
ivi sempre fedele,
l'orme tue seguirà l'alma costante,
e negli abissi ancora,
benché astretto a penar, sarò contento,
pensando alla cagion del mio tormento.

"And wherever, my beloved,
you will turn your steps,
always faithful,
my constant soul will follow your trail,
and even into the abysses,
though compelled to suffer, I will be content,
thinking of the reason for my torment.

4. Aria

"Se penso al caro ben
è troppo, o Dio d'Amor,

"If I think of my dear one
it is too much, O God of Love,

la gioia del mio cor,	the joy of my heart,
il mio contento.	my contentment.
E già dentro al mio sen	And already within my breast
palesa il suo goder	enjoyment is manifest
e per il gran piacer	and in my great delight
brillar mi sento.	I feel myself shining.

5. Recitativo

"E mai lungi da te, bell'idol mio,
non partirà quest'alma
finché mossa a pietade
di chi tanto t'adora
almeno non dirai,
'Ah, che Tirsi è fedele
e sì gran fede io non conobbi mai.'

"And never far from you, my idol,
will my soul take its leave
until you, moved to mercy
for the one who adores you
will not say at least,
'Ah, that Tirsi is faithful
and never did I know such faith.'

6. Aria

"Fu costante di Tirsi la fede,
e Filli non vede
maggior fedeltà.
'Con un cor che mi fu sì fedele
fui troppo crudele
negando pietà.'

"Tirsi's loyalty was constant,
and Filli never saw
greater constancy.
'With a heart that was so loyal to me
I was too cruel
in denying mercy.'

7. Recitativo

"Così pentita allora
della tua crudeltà,
s'amarme non volesti,
d'amar la fede mia risolverai,
ma per voler d'Amore
amarla non potrai.

"Thus repentant
of your cruelty,
if you were not willing to love me,
you will resolve to love my faithfulness,
but for Love's will
you will not be able to love it.

8. Aria

"Amerai, ma sol quell'ombra
che d'intorno a te s'aggira,
e il tuo amor non sentirà.
Ma al mio sen che te sospira
quel dolor ch'il cor gl'ingombra
l'amor tuo non porterà."

"You will love, but only that shade
which hovers around you,
and which will not feel your love.
But to my breast that sighs for you
that pain that encumbers my heart
will not transport your love."

Text edited and translated by Barbara Sachs.

Era l'oscura notte
Serenata a voce sola con strumenti

1. [Recitativo]

Era l'oscura notte e d'ogni intorno di fosco ammanto il ciel si ricopria, quasi che far volesse con quei bruni apparati una pompa funebre al morto giorno, quando, quando

Edited by Rosalind Halton

un mi- se- ro a- man- te, per far pa- le- se la co- stan- te fe- de del- l'a- mo- -ro- so co- re al- l'in- cre- du- la Fil- li che fi- do no 'l cre- de- a,

A tempo largo

la- gri- man- do, so- spi- ran- do, tra la- gri- me e so- spir, tra

2. Aria

la- gri- me e so- spir___ co- sì,___ co- sì di- ce- a.

"Lo ve- drai s'io son fe-

-de- le o cru- de- le, cru- de- le, cru- de- le quan- do l'al- ma in- na- mo- ra- ta dal mio pet- to fug- gi- rà. Lo ve- drai s'io son fe- de- le, lo ve-

175

-drai s'io son fe- de- le o cru- de- le, cru- de- le,

cru- de- le quan- do l'al- ma in na- mo- ra- ta dal mio

pet- to fug- gi- rà.

Per-ché sem- pre a te d'in- tor- no

[Fine]

not- te e gior- no, da' miei spir- ti a- gi-

Presto

-ta- ta, om-bra an-cor s'ag- gi- re- rà, om-bra an-cor s'ag- gi- re- rà, om-bra an-cor s'ag- gi- re- rà, om-bra an-cor s'ag- gi- re- rà.

"Lo ve-drai s'io son fe-

[Dal segno al fine]

3. Recitativo

"E dove, amato bene, tu volgerai le piante, ivi sempre fedele, l'orme tue seguirà l'alma costante, e negli abissi ancora, benché a stretto a penar, sarò contento, pensando alla cagion del mio tormento.

4. Aria

[Violini] all'unisoni

"Se penso al caro ben è troppo o Dio d'A- -mor, è troppo o Dio d'A-mor, la gioia del mio cor, la gioia del mio cor, il mio contento.

Se penso al caro ben è troppo, o Dio d'Amor, è troppo, o Dio d'Amor, la gioia del mio cor, il mio contento. Se penso al caro ben è troppo, o Dio d'Amor, è troppo, o Dio d'A-[mor], la gioia del mio cor, il mio contento.

E già den- tro al mio sen pa- le- sa il suo go- der,

[Fine]

e già den- tro al mio sen— pa- le- sa il suo— go- der— e per— il gran pia-

-cer— bril- lar— mi sen- to, e per— il gran pia- cer— bril- lar— mi sen-

-to. E già den- tro al mio sen— pa- le- sa il suo— go- der,— pa- le- sa il suo go-

-der— e per il gran pia- cer— bril- lar— mi sen- to, bril- lar— mi sen- to. "Se

[Dal segno al fine]

5. Recitativo

"E mai lungi da te, bell'idol mio, non partirà quest'alma finché mossa a pietade di chi tanto t'adora almeno non dirai, 'Ah, che Tirsi è fedele e si gran fede io non conobbi mai.'

6. Aria

Allegro

"Fu costante di Tirsi la fede, e Filli non vede mag-

-gior___ fe- del-tà, e Fil- li non ve- de mag- gior fe- del-tà.

Fu co- stan- te di Tir- si la fe- de, e Fil- li non ve- de, e

Fil- li non ve- de mag-gior fe- del- tà. Fu co- stan- te di Tir- si la fe- de, e

Fil- li non ve- de, e Fil- li non ve- de mag- gior fe- del- tà.

[Fine–Ritornello]

'Con un cor che mi fu sì fe- de- le,

con un cor che mi fu sì fe- de- le fui trop- po cru- de- le, cru- de- le, fui trop- po ne- gan- do pie- tà, fui trop- po cru- de- le ne- gan- do pie- tà, fui trop- po cru- de- le ne- gan- do pie- tà.' "Fu co-

[Dal segno al fine]

Ritornello

7. Recitativo

"Co- sì pen- ti- ta_al- lo- ra del- la tua cru- del- tà, s'a- mar- me non vo- le- sti, d'a- mar la fe- de mi- a ri- sol- ve- ra- i, ma per vo- ler d'A- mo- re a- mar- la non po- tra- i.

8. Aria

Allegro

"A- me- rai, ma sol quel- l'om- bra che d'in- tor- no_a te

s'ag- gi- ra, e il tuo a- mor, no, no,__ non__ sen- ti- rà.

A- me- rai, ma sol quel- -l'om- bra che__ d'in- tor- no a te__ s'ag- gi- ra,

*See critical note.

Ma al mio sen che te sospira quel dolor ch'il cor gl'in- gom- bra l'a- mor tuo no, no, non por- te- rà, l'a- mor tuo no, no, non por- te- rà, non por- te- rà." "A- me-

[Fine]

[Dal segno al fine]

FINE

Source

There is one extant source of *Era l'oscura notte*:

Münster, Santini-Bibliothek (D-MÜs), Hs. 3938. Watermark: fleur-de-lys in a double circle. Title information: "Serenata | A voce sola | con Viol.ni" (title page) and "Serenata a voce sola con Strum.ti" (first page of music). The manuscript contains only the single work. Copyist: Rome, Copyist XIII in Watanabe's identification scheme; see note 2 of "The Authorship of *Era l'oscura notte*."

Critical Notes

1. [Recitativo]

M. 7, V, notes 4–5 are c″–b♭′, conflicting with Vn. 2 part which preserves ascending pattern, cf. m. 5. M. 10, Vn. 1, beats 3–4, part doubles voice, crossed out. M. 12, V, note 4 is lacking; 8th note added in edition to make up required number of syllables ("fe-de"). M. 18, erasures in B. part.

2. Aria

M. 2, Vn. 1, note 4 is b♭′, but c″ in recurrence of passage in m. 26. M. 37, V part is written in Vn. 2 stave, then erased, so that the Vn. 2 part is obscure here; an editorial note e♭″ resolves the cadence from m. 36 as the third of the chord, by analogy with mm. 20 and 35. M. 38, Vn. 1, entry marked *Presto*. M. 46, *D. Capo* with vocal cue and segno.

4. Aria

M. 1, *All'unisono* for violin stave. Mm. 53–54 and 54–55, V, text is "dolor"; edition uses "goder" as seen in mm. 40–41 and 47–48. M. 58, *D. Capo* with vocal cue and segno.

6. Aria

Mm. 2–3, B., 8th notes are undotted, but m. 4 and elsewhere the same ritornello music is dotted, e.g., mm. 25–27, including the ritornello following the aria; undotted 8th notes occur only at the setting of "e Filli non vede" in mm. 9–10 (and following in B., m. 12). Mm. 17 and 22, V, slur appears to be over notes 5–6 (i.e., from beat 3 to beat 4), but the more obvious slurring and underlay of notes within beat 3 follows m. 10. M. 44, the source writes out the da capo repeat with beats moved, i.e., beat 1 of m. 6 becomes beat 3 of m. 44; a compensating bar and a half (see mm. 6–7 with added segno) reestablishes the barring pattern. M. 48, Vn. 1, note 6 is g″. M. 51, Vn. 1, beat 4 begins with quarter rest; edition follows m. 56 and V, mm. 14 and 19. M. 54, Vn. 1, note 4 is e″ (cf. phrase repetition, m. 59).

8. Aria

Mm. 25, 81, and 97, V, placement of syllables is unclear in source; short-long pattern is adopted in edition, cf. wordsetting in mm. 27 and 42. Mm. 48–55, a "petite reprise" before the ritornello is signalled by double *SS* with dots on either side, placed above the vocal stave and below the bass; in the edition, these are notated as modern repeat bars. M. 91, Vn. 1, note 6 is b♭′. M. 97, *D. Capo* with vocal cue and segno.

Recent Researches in the Music of the Baroque Era
Steven Saunders, general editor

Vol.	Composer: Title
1	Marc-Antoine Charpentier: *Judicium Salomonis*
2	Georg Philipp Telemann: *Forty-eight Chorale Preludes*
3	Johann Caspar Kerll: *Missa Superba*
4–5	Jean-Marie Leclair: *Sonatas for Violin and Basso continuo, Opus 5*
6	*Ten Eighteenth-Century Voluntaries*
7–8	William Boyce: *Two Anthems for the Georgian Court*
9	Giulio Caccini: *Le nuove musiche*
10–11	Jean-Marie Leclair: *Sonatas for Violin and Basso continuo, Opus 9 and Opus 15*
12	Johann Ernst Eberlin: *Te Deum; Dixit Dominus; Magnificat*
13	Gregor Aichinger: *Cantiones Ecclesiasticae*
14–15	Giovanni Legrenzi: *Cantatas and Canzonets for Solo Voice*
16	Giovanni Francesco Anerio and Francesco Soriano: *Two Settings of Palestrina's "Missa Papae Marcelli"*
17	Giovanni Paolo Colonna: *Messe a nove voci concertata con stromenti*
18	Michel Corrette: *"Premier livre d'orgue" and "Nouveau livre de noëls"*
19	Maurice Greene: *Voluntaries and Suites for Organ and Harpsichord*
20	Giovanni Antonio Piani: *Sonatas for Violin Solo and Violoncello with Cembalo*
21–22	Marin Marais: *Six Suites for Viol and Thoroughbass*
23–24	Dario Castello: *Selected Ensemble Sonatas*
25	*A Neapolitan Festa a Ballo and Selected Instrumental Ensemble Pieces*
26	Antonio Vivaldi: *The Manchester Violin Sonatas*
27	Louis-Nicolas Clérambault: *Two Cantatas for Soprano and Chamber Ensemble*
28	Giulio Caccini: *Nuove musiche e nuova maniera di scriverle (1614)*
29–30	Michel Pignolet de Montéclair: *Cantatas for One and Two Voices*
31	Tomaso Albinoni: *Twelve Cantatas, Opus 4*
32–33	Antonio Vivaldi: *Cantatas for Solo Voice*
34	Johann Kuhnau: *Magnificat*
35	Johann Stadlmayr: *Selected Magnificats*
36–37	Jacopo Peri: *Euridice: An Opera in One Act, Five Scenes*
38	Francesco Severi: *Salmi passaggiati (1615)*
39	George Frideric Handel: *Six Concertos for the Harpsichord or Organ (Walsh's Transcriptions, 1738)*
40	*The Brasov Tablature (Brasov Music Manuscript 808): German Keyboard Studies 1608–1684*
41	John Coprario: *Twelve Fantasias for Two Bass Viols and Organ and Eleven Pieces for Three Lyra Viols*

42	Antonio Cesti: *Il pomo d'oro (Music for Acts III and V from Modena, Biblioteca Estense, Ms. Mus. E. 120)*
43	Tomaso Albinoni: *Pimpinone: Intermezzi comici musicali*
44–45	Antonio Lotti: *Duetti, terzetti, e madrigali a piu voci*
46	Matthias Weckmann: *Four Sacred Concertos*
47	Jean Gilles: *Requiem (Messe des morts)*
48	Marc-Antoine Charpentier: *Vocal Chamber Music*
49	*Spanish Art Song in the Seventeenth Century*
50	Jacopo Peri: *"Le varie musiche" and Other Songs*
51–52	Tomaso Albinoni: *Sonatas and Suites, Opus 8, for Two Violins, Violoncello, and Basso continuo*
53	Agostino Steffani: *Twelve Chamber Duets*
54–55	Gregor Aichinger: *The Vocal Concertos*
56	Giovanni Battista Draghi: *Harpsichord Music*
57	*Concerted Sacred Music of the Bologna School*
58	Jean-Marie Leclair: *Sonatas for Violin and Basso continuo, Opus 2*
59	Isabella Leonarda: *Selected Compositions*
60–61	Johann Schelle: *Six Chorale Cantatas*
62	Denis Gaultier: *La Rhétorique des Dieux*
63	Marc-Antoine Charpentier: *Music for Molière's Comedies*
64–65	Georg Philipp Telemann: *Don Quichotte auf der Hochzeit des Comacho: Comic Opera-Serenata in One Act*
66	Henry Butler: *Collected Works*
67–68	John Jenkins: *The Lyra Viol Consorts*
69	*Keyboard Transcriptions from the Bach Circle*
70	Melchior Franck: *Geistliche Gesäng und Melodeyen*
71	Georg Philipp Telemann: *Douze solos, à violon ou traversière*
72	Marc-Antoine Charpentier: *Nine Settings of the "Litanies de la Vierge"*
73	*The Motets of Jacob Praetorius II*
74	Giovanni Porta: *Selected Sacred Music from the Ospedale della Pietà*
75	*Fourteen Motets from the Court of Ferdinand II of Hapsburg*
76	Jean-Marie Leclair: *Sonatas for Violin and Basso continuo, Opus 1*
77	Antonio Bononcini: *Complete Sonatas for Violoncello and Basso continuo*
78	Christoph Graupner: *Concerti Grossi for Two Violins*
79	Paolo Quagliati: *Il primo libro de' madrigali a quattro voci*
80	Melchior Franck: *Dulces Mundani Exilij Deliciae*
81	*Late-Seventeenth-Century English Keyboard Music*
82	*Solo Compositions for Violin and Viola da gamba with Basso continuo*
83	Barbara Strozzi: *Cantate, ariete a una, due e tre voci, Opus 3*
84	Charles-Hubert Gervais: *Super flumina Babilonis*
85	Henry Aldrich: *Selected Anthems and Motet Recompositions*

86	Lodovico Grossi da Viadana: *Salmi a quattro cori*
87	Chiara Margarita Cozzolani: *Motets*
88	Elisabeth-Claude Jacquet de La Guerre: *Cephale et Procris*
89	Sébastien Le Camus: *Airs à deux et trois parties*
90	Thomas Ford: *Lyra Viol Duets*
91	*Dedication Service for St. Gertrude's Chapel, Hamburg, 1607*
92	Johann Klemm: *Partitura seu Tabulatura italica*
93	Giovanni Battista Somis: *Sonatas for Violin and Basso continuo, Opus 3*
94	John Weldon: *The Judgment of Paris*
95–96	Juan Bautista Comes: *Masses. Parts 1–2*
97	Sebastian Knüpfer: *Lustige Madrigalien und Canzonetten*
98	Stefano Landi: *La morte d'Orfeo*
99	Giovanni Battista Fontana: *Sonatas for One, Two, and Three Parts with Basso continuo*
100	Georg Philipp Telemann: *Twelve Trios*
101	Fortunato Chelleri: *Keyboard Music*
102	Johann David Heinichen: *La gara degli Dei*
103	Johann David Heinichen: *Diana su l'Elba*
104	Alessandro Scarlatti: *Venere, Amore e Ragione*
105	*Songs with Theorbo (ca. 1650–1663)*
106	Melchior Franck: *Paradisus Musicus*
107	Heinrich Ignaz Franz von Biber: *Missa Christi resurgentis*
108	Johann Ludwig Bach: *Motets*
109–10	Giovanni Rovetta: *Messa, e salmi concertati, op. 4 (1639). Parts 1–2*
111	Johann Joachim Quantz: *Seven Trio Sonatas*
112	Petits motets *from the Royal Convent School at Saint Cyr*
113	Isabella Leonarda: *Twelve Sonatas, Opus 16*
114	Rudolph di Lasso: *Virginalia Eucharistica (1615)*
115	Giuseppe Torelli: *Concerti musicali, Opus 6*
116–17	Nicola Francesco Haym: *Complete Sonatas. Parts 1–2*
118	Benedetto Marcello: *Il pianto e il riso delle quattro stagioni*
119	Loreto Vittori: *La Galatea*
120–23	William Lawes: *Collected Vocal Music. Parts 1–4*
124	Marco da Gagliano: *Madrigals. Part 1*
125	Johann Schop: *Erster Theil newer Paduanen*
126	Giovanni Felice Sances: *Motetti a una, due, tre, e quattro voci (1638)*
127	Thomas Elsbeth: *Sontägliche Evangelien*
128–30	Giovanni Antonio Rigatti: *Messa e salmi, parte concertati. Parts 1–3*
131	*Seventeenth-Century Lutheran Church Music with Trombones*
132	Francesco Cavalli: *La Doriclea*

133	*Music for "Macbeth"*
134	Domenico Allegri: *Music for an Academic Defense (Rome, 1617)*
135	Jean Gilles: *Diligam te, Domine*
136	Silvius Leopold Weiss: *Lute Concerti*
137	*Masses by Alessandro Scarlatti and Francesco Gasparini*
138	Giovanni Ghizzolo: *Madrigali et arie per sonare et cantare*
139	Michel Lambert: *Airs from "Airs de différents autheurs"*
140	William Babell: *Twelve Solos for a Violin or Oboe with Basso Continuo. Book 1*
141	Giovanni Francesco Anerio: *Selva armonica (Rome, 1617)*
142–43	Bellerofonte Castaldi: *Capricci (1622). Parts 1–2*
144	Georg von Bertouch: *Sonatas a 3*
145	Marco da Gagliano: *Madrigals. Part 2*
146	Giovanni Rovetta: *Masses*
147	Giacomo Antonio Perti: *Five-Voice Motets for the Assumption of the Virgin Mary*
148	Giovanni Felice Sances: *Motetti a 2, 3, 4, e cinque voci (1642)*
149	*La grand-mére amoureuse, parodie d'Atys*
150	Andreas Hammerschmidt: *Geistlicher Dialogen Ander Theil*
151	Georg von Bertouch: *Three Sacred Cantatas*
152	Giovanni Maria Ruggieri: *Two Settings of the Gloria*
153	Alessandro Scarlatti: *Concerti sacri, opera seconda*
154	Johann Sigismund Kusser: *Adonis*
155	John Blow: *Selected Verse Anthems*
156	Anton Holzner: *Viretum pierium (1621)*
157	Alessandro Scarlatti: *Venere, Adone, et Amore*
158	Marc-Antoine Charpentier: *In nativitatem Domini canticum, H. 416*
159	Francesco Scarlatti: *Six Concerti Grossi*
160	Charles Avison: *Concerto Grosso Arrangements of Geminiani's Opus 1 Violin Sonatas*
161	Johann David Heinichen: *Selected Music for Vespers*
162–63	Francesco Gasparini: *Cantatas with Violins. Parts 1–2*
164–65	Antoine Boesset: *Sacred Music. Parts 1–2*
166	Andreas Hammerschmidt: *Selections from the "Gespräche" (1655–56) with Capellen*
167	Santiago de Murcia: *Cifras selectas de guitarra*
168	Gottfried Heinrich Stölzel: *German Te Deum*
169	Biagio Marini: *Compositioni varie per musica di camera, Opus 13*
170	Santiago Billoni: *Complete Works*
171	Marco da Gagliano: *La Flora*
172	Girolamo Polani: *Six Chamber Cantatas for Solo Voice*
173	Bonifazio Graziani: *Motets for Two to Six Voices, Opus 1*
174	Marco da Gagliano: *Madrigals. Part 3*
175	Alessandro Scarlatti: *Solo Serenatas*

GREYSCALE

BIN TRAVELER FORM

Cut By Alonso #11   Qty 15   Date 02.10.26

Scanned By_____ Qty_____ Date_____

Scanned Batch ID's

Notes/Exception